The term 'cybernetics' was first coined in 1947 by Norbert Wiener to describe a phenomenon as old as life in nature, and as recent in the man-made world as the digital computer. Any system that responds to its environment—man, steam engine, computer, thermostat, political system, automated factory—can be described as a cybernetic system.

Maurice Trask shows how cybernetics and the ideas of communication and control can be applied to every aspect of life. He takes the story from the beginning of history, from man's first attempts to understand the world around him, to count and calculate with sand tables and notches in tally sticks, to the sophisticated inventions of the nineteenth century such as Babbage's Analytical Engine and Kelvin's Tide Predictor, which needed only the greater resources of twentieth-century society to develop into the electronic computers we know today. Did you know that you are a cybernetic system? If you didn't then this fascinating book will teach you something about yourself as well as the world at large.

The Story of Cybernetics is a revised and extended version of the display first produced by IBM for the highly successful exhibition 'Cybernetic Serendipity' at the Institute of Contemporary Arts, London, which showed how the principles discussed in this book can be applied to the creative arts.

Maurice Trask is exhibition and display adviser for IBM United Kingdom Limited, has been closely associated with the computer industry since 1955 and has designed a number of major exhibitions for IBM.

Front cover: a diagram of the inside of Vaucanson's duck

Back cover: a replica of Charles Babbage's Difference Engine

The story of cybernetics

Maurice Trask

The story of cybernetics

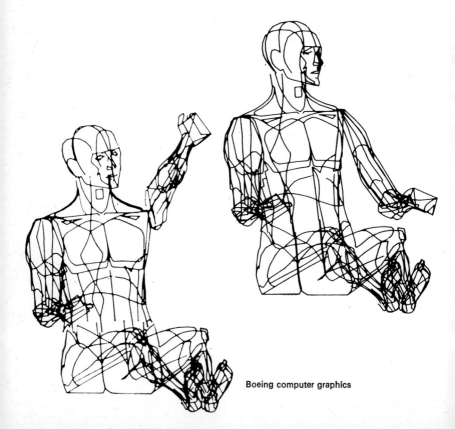

Boeing computer graphics

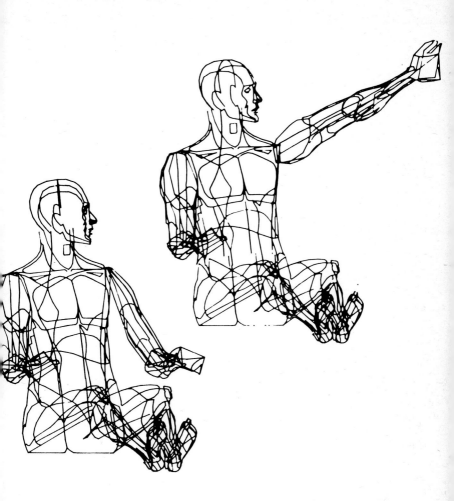

Studio Vista | Dutton Pictureback

General Editor David Herbert

© Institute of Contemporary Arts, London 1971
Designed by Gillian Greenwood
Published in Great Britain by Studio Vista Limited
Blue Star House, Highgate Hill, London N19
and in the USA by E. P. Dutton and Co., Inc.
201 Park Avenue South, New York, NY 10003
Set in 8D on 11 pt Univers 689
Made and printed in Great Britain by
Richard Clay (The Chaucer Press), Ltd, Bungay, Suffolk

SBN 289 70057 4 (paperback)
     289 70058 2 (cased)

Contents

Steersman on a Greek ship, from a clay plaque *c.* 700 BC

Control

Cybernetics. 'Control and communication in the animal and the machine.' (Norbert Wiener)

'Cybernetics' is one of those strange words that find their way into the English language from the fields of science, without our really understanding what they mean. With 'electronics' and 'computer' it stands for ideas and things which are having a revolutionary effect on our daily lives. Where did it come from and what does it mean?

There have been many attempts to arrive at a meaning since Wiener's first and classic definition. For some it means automation, or the application of computers, to others it suggests making 'robots' that imitate man and animals.

The idea of control is at the root of cybernetics. All human action is 'controlled' either because we choose to do something and make whatever moves we must to do it, or because for our our safety we make some automatic or reflex action, like pulling away from something hot. The Greeks had a word for it: κυβερνητης *kubernetes*, meaning steersman, helmsman; root of the English word to govern, hence to rule, regulate, control. A seafaring nation, like the Greeks or the British, would know that the man who steers a ship is 'in control'. The skill used in steering, or performing any action, is one of continuous judgment. The helmsman must keep control, or his ship will go on the rocks. How is this undesirable end avoided? The helmsman continually adjusts his tiller to keep the boat on course. He observes any variation from his course, estimates the adjustment needed to overcome it, moves the tiller, observes the result and repeats the process.

Any action directed towards a goal must be controlled to achieve that goal. Progress of the action at any moment cannot be known without some form of communication. The two functions of control and communication are necessary for any systematic action, voluntary or involuntary.

We control by minimizing error—for any course of action is

Gull hovering before landing : control in the animal

a series of approximations. The helmsman corrects the error resulting from his previous attempt to correct a previous error. At the same time he must compensate for the effect of wind, current, speed and their resultant forces on hull and rudder.

Helicopter in hovering flight: man controlling a machine

These are the basic principles of cybernetics. Helmsman, bird and automatic pilot use the same principle in different ways. But they are all doing something which is complicated even though it looks simple.

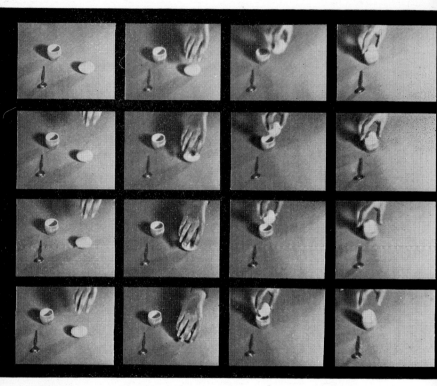

Cycle of movements started by the intention 'to pick up the egg'. From a film sequence

Opposite
Without feedback the egg would be crushed ... or forever out of reach

Now try an experiment: imagine you have to pick up an egg and put it in a nearby egg cup. Your hand moves towards the egg, your body corrects its balance, your fingers grasp the egg, without breaking it, and put it in the egg cup. You have not consciously told each muscle what to do, only set a goal to pick up the egg, yet some of the actions, such as grasping the egg firmly enough to lift it without breaking the shell, are

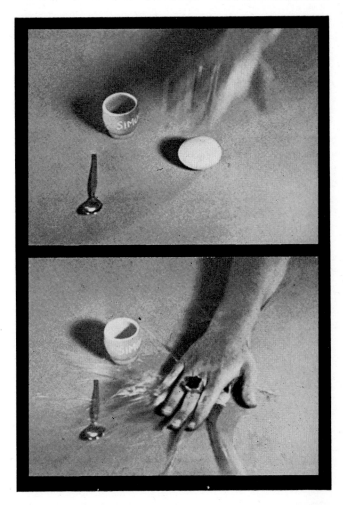

surprisingly delicate. The movement of your hand is regulated by feedback (a message reporting the effect of action), without which the egg would be crushed, or forever out of reach.

When you first reach towards the egg your arm must be guided to close the gap between hand and egg until they touch. The messages from senses to nervous system, which we have called feedback, report the extent to which your hand has failed to reach the egg. Other messages from the nervous system to muscles instruct them to act. The muscles use energy to move nearer to the egg and the whole cycle is repeated until the egg is reached.

The senses and nervous system we call an 'information' system which carries reports and instructions; the muscles we call an 'energy' system which does the work. Cybernetics is the study and use of information systems to regulate energy systems.

Let us compare the egg problem with a similar one—a man using a machine. All motorists have parking problems, how to fit a valuable car into a limited space without damage to it, and preferably without visible damage to its near neighbours. Now assume the driver cannot easily see front or back bumper, but has an obliging passenger to act as his eyes. From the pavement the passenger watches the car back towards one neighbour, signals or shouts any necessary alterations like 'stop!' or 'right lock'. On receiving his instructions the driver translates them into machine instruction by braking, changing gear or steering. The car provides the energy to move or stop moving.

Here the passenger acts as a sensor, his signals or shouts act as messages; the driver is the receiver, and because he puts the messages into action he is also called an effector. Together they form the information system, the car the energy system.

Now suppose the car in front starts to pull out. The situation immediately changes and a decision has to be taken, either continue to park as before or wait until the other car has gone and drive straight into its space. The car could not take this decision, nor could a simple machine designed say to rock to and fro until it had fitted into the desired position. But the man/car combination is able to change its course of action to suit new circumstances.

The most often quoted example of feedback is the heating system. Put a heater in a room and leave it switched on. Without control it will continue to add heat to the room until a sweating occupant turns it off, when the heat will drop until the outside temperature is reached. This is an open loop which has no means of controlling itself to adapt to required conditions.

Now add a thermostat which can switch off at a set high temperature, and on again at some lower temperature. The system can control itself to the extent that when the top limit is reached the thermostat switches off, and cuts in again when the temperature drops below the set level. This is a closed loop, using

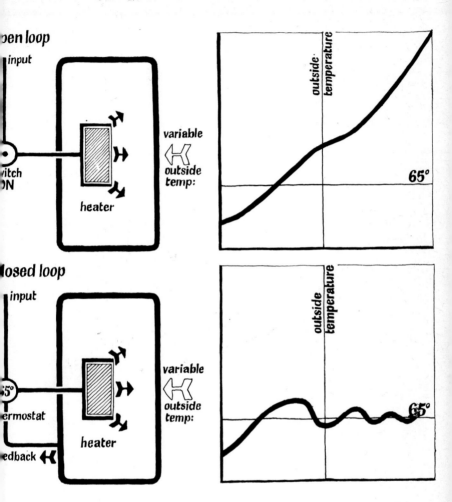

open loop

input

switch
ON

heater

variable
outside
temp:

outside temperature

65°

closed loop

input

65°
thermostat

feedback

heater

variable
outside
temp:

outside temperature

65°

Room heating control: the difference between an open loop and a closed
loop system, with feedback through a thermostat

15

Cybernetic systems

feedback through the thermostat to achieve control. A closed loop oscillates between limits and can be designed to get closer and closer to the temperature required. The heating can also adapt to changed conditions outside the room to keep a steady temperature. This self-regulation by feedback, the 'closed loop', is found in all cybernetic processes—living, natural, mechanical or social.

Cybernetic systems

The idea of control can be applied to a great many processes that are neither living nor mechanical in the accepted sense, but can be thought of as behaving like a self-regulating machine. Studious children, living animals, political system, production line, moving traffic, electronic computer, gathering storm, Stock Exchange: the common factor—all are cybernetic systems.

The information cycle

'To live effectively is to live with adequate information.
(Norbert Wiener)

The popularity of quiz games a few years ago indicated that many people collect what is commonly called 'useless knowledge'. To know how many one-legged men crossed the Niagara Falls in 1901 might win a prize, but its value as information is at least suspect. But what is adequate information? In the context of this book it is knowing just enough to take a decision. Too little and the decision cannot be taken, too much and the alternatives may cause indecision. Wrong or distorted information can produce a wrong decision.

Sir Winston Churchill once observed that we know more about Alfred the Great than we do of Garibaldi, simply because there is so much recorded conflicting information about Garibaldi's life.

Before we look at the cycle by which the information necessary to cybernetic systems is collected and used, a further look at feedback is necessary. Things like spoons, stones, books or motor cars do not use feedback, they cannot act without outside forces. They are 'docile' machines. A rolling stone hits a wall because it cannot sense or anticipate the wall's presence. A human runner would see such an unexpected obstacle and react by jumping over or going around it. The spoon cracks the egg only as a tool of the controlling hand.

Docile machines then are the tools of cybernetic systems, unable to act by themselves, except as open-loop machines when some kind of mechanism is involved. This group includes most early automata which were mechanical systems with a fixed program, unable to modify it yet appearing to act like cybernetic systems. The general significance of the idea of feedback was noted by Wilhelm Gottfried von Leibniz (1646–1716). In his theory of the way the universe is organized, feedback always keeps the universe in an optimum state. This is negative feedback, any

With a definite goal to achieve the athlete may literally take obstacles in his stride in order to reach it

Head of a fly: sensors adapted to very different needs from our own

◀ The uncertain wobble of a learner cyclist is far removed from the skilled
balance, steering and muscle-control of the racing cyclist

change or error is opposed by the action of the control system
which acts to maintain the original condition. That we learn by
our mistakes is a common saying which describes the effect of
negative feedback. Without it we could not learn to walk, ride a
bicycle, throw a dart or write. The first mistake would be repeated
indefinitely.

All animals get their feedback through their senses or receptors.
Sight, hearing, touch, taste, smell tell us all we know of the
outside world. The special sense organs—eyes, ears, nose—
transmit vast quantities of information to the central nervous

General scheme of thirty pairs of spinal nerves, from *De Humani Corporis Fabrica*, Andreas Vesalius (1514–64)

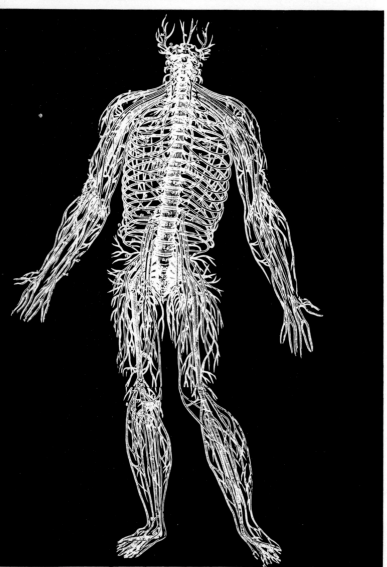

system. Nerve-endings on the body's surface also send back messages, reporting sensations like temperature and pressure in a continuous stream. All this information is reduced to quantities the brain can handle, by eliminating redundancy and using temporary storage to be retrieved or discarded later.

In movement kinaesthetic senses monitor the performance of joints and muscles, the effectors. Nerve impulses to muscle plates cause contraction according to frequency of impulse, strain receptors feed back the degree of contraction. The visual sense also returns signals for the same action, so the two kinds of sense act as a two loop servomechanism.

Servomechanism is another word for feedback loop, and comes from the Latin for 'slave'. The characteristics of a servosystem are those of the information cycle used for measuring, usually to control mechanical movement. The servomotor is the power amplifier to convert instruction into movement.

Within the body homeostasis is the survival mechanism, a hierarchy of feedback systems regulating the organs, glands and states of the body to remain stable. The body's need for stable conditions, like heart beat, body temperature, sugar level, are controlled by involuntary systems which react to changes of internal and external conditions.

IBM Selectric typewriter: the keys sense a finger touch and send instructions to select the equivalent letter on the printing head

Railway tracks form a complex system of channels and switches resembling computer circuitry in operation

Mechanical, natural and social systems also have their senses. The opinion poll, election centres and protest demonstrations are sensors of social change. Chemical reactions or atmospheric movements are sensors in natural systems.

Many human senses can be imitated by man-made sensors, called transducers—thermostat, strain gauge, photoelectric cell, microphone—to provide feedback for automatic systems.

All sensors and transducers send coded messages or signals. These coded signals can take many forms, such as electrical pulses, sound waves, chemical changes, light flashes, indeed any change of state which can be transmitted in some way is a signal. These signals can be measured, so information can be handled in mathematical terms much as a physical quantity like mass or energy.

Signals then are coded information sent along a communication channel, which is any link between a transmitter and a receiver—nerve fibre, electric wire, radiowave, postal system, pneumatic tube, motorway—all are channels. For example, the morse code is a sequence of signals which can be sent by radio, smoke signal, flashing light or water pipe.

Interference can distort or interrupt a signal. The radio programme that is difficult to listen to, conversation in a crowd, and morse code flashes in a fog are all subject to 'noise', as interference is called. Noise can be a great problem in communication, because distorted information may be misinterpreted, and it is

Motorway and railway : communication channels which dominate the urban landscape they serve

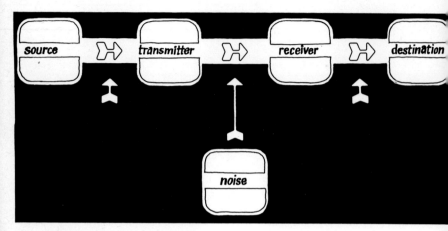

Elements of a communication system

often necessary to go to great lengths to prevent it, to check the quality of the signal or even to reconstruct it. In photography it is now possible to show a badly exposed or fogged photograph to a computer system, which will analyse and reconstruct it as a clear image. A similar process was used to clarify moon shots from the Apollo spacecraft.

Signals are either continuous, like the electric current in a car thermometer cable, or in pulses as the morse code. To decode the information we measure the continuous signals or count the individual pulses. All information is received in one of these ways. In everything that measures or counts we use analog and digital methods, probably without realizing it.

To measure we compare an unknown quantity with one we already know, like a length marked as a ruler. An analogy is drawn between them, so this way of measuring is an 'analog'.

To count we separate each part and give it a number, or digit, in sequence. This one to one correspondence is 'digital'.

To reason about this information we follow sets of rules, which are called 'logic'. Mathematics is the logic which handles quantities.

The analog as a measure of size operates when you stand on a weighing machine, the pointer swings across the scale to stop at your weight. That position on the scale is an analog of your

Analogs

The sandglass, using a volume of sand
to measure time

The weighing machine, using length
to measure weight

The half-tone photograph:

Above: continuous gradations of tone representing variations of light intensity

Left: the same photograph with a dot screen which converts an analog to a digital form of the same image

weight, since one physical variable, weight, is imitated by another, length. Such measurements are continuously variable, merging imperceptibly from one to the next. The accuracy with which we can read the measurements limits their precision.

The astronomical clock at Hampton Court: an analog of celestial movement. Clocks may be analog or digital, depending on the type of movement, but are usually read as if they were digital

The digital counting of quantities is more easy to recognize, since we use numbers or number patterns to identify groups of objects—two lovely black eyes, five-finger exercises, the twelve days of Christmas—in which each unit keeps its separate identity.

If you number off all the pages in this book, starting with one, you would be using this digital counting process. Each individual page is distinct from the next and the change from one to the next is at least one step or digit. The word digit comes from the Latin for 'finger'. In counting no matter how small the step there is always a jump from one to the next. This method can be as precise as we need since we can reckon to as many places as is necessary.

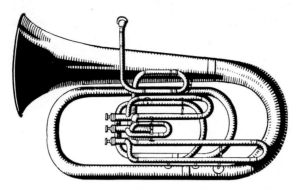

Tuba: one of a number of musical instruments which play notes at fixed intervals, and, therefore, are digital

Child's bricks: an early introduction to discrete objects and counting

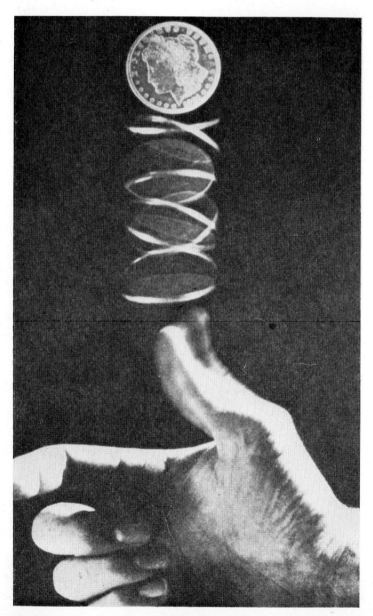

The toss of a coin : a choice between two equal probabilities, heads or tails, with a probability of 0·5

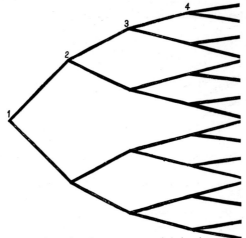

Binary diagram of the alternative paths when a sequence of choices is followed, as in the game of 'Twenty Questions'

The meaning or content of the information being sent through a communication channel does not matter until it reaches a receiver and is decoded in a form the receiver can use. The radio wave does not 'know' whether it is carrying a political tirade or a symphony concert, neither for that matter does the air which transmits the sound from performer to microphone, and from loudspeaker to listener. In information theory the choices made from a set of possible messages is important, not the meaning of the message. This is a statistical process using a series of choices between two possibilities, a probability of 0·5, as the basic series. The information provided by one choice is one binary digit (bit), a measure we shall meet later when looking at computers.

In the 'Twenty Questions' game players have twenty chances to identify one object, starting by knowing nothing. Each question may be answered by 'yes' or 'no' only. By dividing each established fact in halves each time : is it animate (or inanimate) ; is it human (or non-human) ; is it alive (or dead) ; is it male (or female) : then they can arrive at one fact from one million possibilities in twenty questions, that is handle twenty bits of information. Of course they may not succeed, the wrong question asked or an ambiguous result can reduce the game to wild guessing. But the human mind is capable of making intuitive guesses which bypass the sequence of question and answer, so a player can sometimes get the right result from only a few questions.

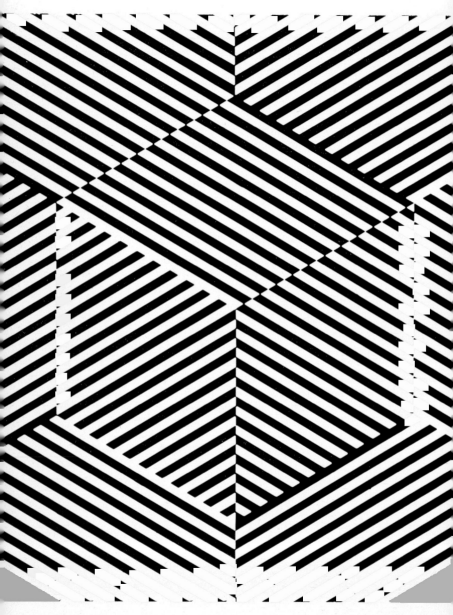

Information conveyed by signals is decoded to become feedback used for control, and is compared with the goal, as when the egg was to be picked up. A decision to either do nothing, correct the error, or start some other action is taken. This is a logic step in the neural network of the brain, or the switching network of the machine.

The information cycle is completed when a quantitative decision is sent along another channel as an instruction to be acted on, like 'move the hand one step nearer the egg'.

The end result, or output, is an action taken by the energy system, muscles or communicating organs in living things, or their equivalent—servomotor, loud-speaker, parliament, raincloud, in other systems. If the effect is sensed as feedback a new cycle begins.

The parts of the cycle will be very different in different systems, but in cybernetics one system can be studied in terms of another. If we know nothing about something we study how it behaves in order to understand it and call it a 'black box'. That intriguing present 'not to be opened until Christmas day' is a 'black box' which the inquisitive child shakes, squeezes, weighs in his hands, examines in every way he can and compares what he finds with other things he already knows. If it squeaks is it another toy duck, a rattle could mean a game or a model kit, something hard and heavy may be a book. Whatever black box we examine, the inputs and outputs can be observed, but the processes by which they are related and controlled are unknown and have to be deduced by making comparisons.

To investigate such systems we construct models in terms of other known systems, compare their outputs with those of the original, and gauge how well our model represents it. We may not need to know how a system works in order to use it. The man feeding his problem to a computer can get an intelligible answer without understanding its circuits or switches.

An optical 'black box' which can take different forms according to our interpretation of sensations received from it

Count, measure, think

The three activities of counting, measuring and reasoning are the
means we use to examine, evaluate, understand and control the
world we live in. From early times man has collected information
about the bewildering variety of natural phenomena around him,
drawn conclusions about their relationships and constructed
'ideas' to explain them. The ability to reason is one of searching for
and recognizing underlying patterns. The development of civilization has come from the communication of these patterns or ideas
between men. If a pattern is found to be inadequate or over
complicated, a new, more satisfactory one must be found. The
search for pattern we now call Science, '. . . organized common
sense; it deals with the orderliness we find in the world' (Norman
Feather, *Mass, Length and Time*).

When man first learned to count we do not know. His needs
were probably simple, as are those of primitive tribes today for
whom 'one, two, many' is adequate. The earliest need was to
survive but man soon learned to make tools to extend his abilities,
to aid his mind as well as his body.

The simple artifacts of early civilization were imprecise. The
accuracy of our watches would have been unimaginable to the
Greeks or Alexandrians, yet they measured the earth and the
heavens, numbered the universe and built elaborate theories on
their observations.

Mathematics is the search for precision, the history of mathematics the mirror of evolving civilization. The size and number
languages had to be manipulated with ever greater accuracy, in an
ever-increasing volume. Speed became important, only machines
could relieve man of the labour of measuring and calculating.
From simple tools to automata the search for mechanical methods
of computation and proof has led to machines which can examine,
evaluate and control, though understanding is as yet beyond their
ability.

Defining the world and dividing the heavens: a variety of ancient measuring instruments

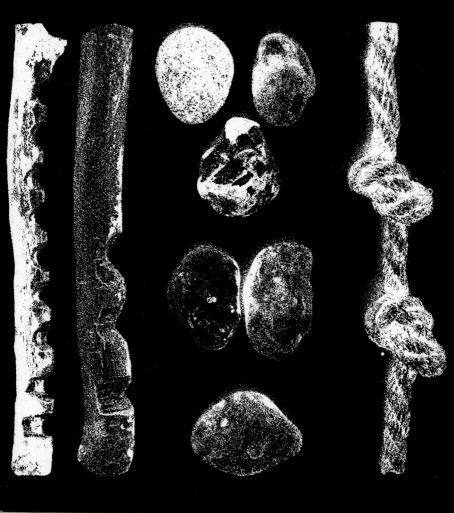

Tally sticks, pebbles, knotted string: early methods of recording quantities

From counting on fingers and measuring with limbs man learned to describe his world in a number language. We retain vestiges of early methods in the 'foot' and the habit of counting in tens. Natural objects—shells, stones, sticks—were conveniently found tools for representing numbers. For records, quantities were

Sand table

scratched on stones, impressed in baked clay, notched in sticks. The earliest calculating device, the sand table, used pebbles in furrows of sand. Our word calculate comes from the Roman *calculus*, a pebble.

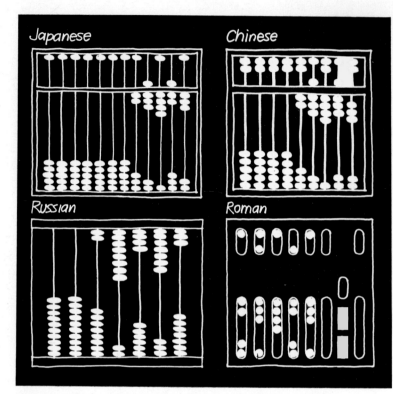

Four types of abacus, each using a different method of recording the same number

Computation is a process of altering symbols according to accepted rules. Each civilization has evolved its own symbols and its own number language. Simple strokes, like notches on a tally stick, suffice for small numbers. The Egyptians grouped numbers in tens and by 3000 BC used hieroglyphs to represent them. Methods of grouping in tens and hundreds are common to most Near East civilizations. Systems using letters of the alphabet are cumbersome for computation and were primarily used to record abacus calculations. The Babylonians used groups of sixty from which we derive our measures of time and angles, but as each unit requires a separate symbol small groups of units are easier to record and manipulate. Our own decimal notation, the so-called

Chinese framed rod and bead abacus: the digits represented, from left to right, 007230189

Arabic numerals, derive from Hindu, Sanskrit and tenth-century Arabic characters.

From the sand table developed the counting frame or abacus, a portable calculator which used beads on sticks, and later a frame with beads on wires or rods, to do positional arithmetic. The abacus seems to have been invented in several separate cultures. Confucian China and Dynastic Egypt knew it, the Romans took it from the Etruscans, the invading Spaniards found it in Pre-Columbian Mexico and Peru. In Russia, Japan and Western Europe it was an every day tool. Yet 3000 years elapsed between the invention of the abacus, which uses a positional decimal notation, and the use of the same notation in written arithmetic.

The abacus was so efficient a tool that written notation served merely to record its results, not for processes of computation.

The efficient system of positional decimals we use came from the Hindus and Arabs, both of whom made little use of the abacus. They gave us also the concept of 'zero', equivalent to the empty rod of the early abacus.

The abacus is the most significant aid to computation ever invented, for centuries it was the only manual calculator in use. Today the simple bead abacus is still used and in skilled hands it can be as fast as a desk calculator.

The notion of time is probably one of the earliest of human concepts and is central to our existence. The measurement of time is based on our experience of the constancy of recurring events. The wandering tribes of early men observed the heavens; rites, rituals and settled city life called for a calendar and a time keeper, so the first accurate measures were celestial fixes on the stars and the sun.

Precise astronomical observations preceded both land surveying and tax gathering as a stimulus to accurate measurement. The method of fixing the north-south meridian and the equinoxes was known before the calendar civilizations began. Festivals were fixed by the sun's position and many ancient monuments were sited to fix solstices by the alignment of pillars and the sun. Stonehenge, Mayan calendar temples, the pyramids and obelisks, all relate to the angular measure of stars or the sun.

Stonehenge: a vast astronomical computer for predicting equinoxes, solstices, eclipses of sun and moon, and celestial cycles

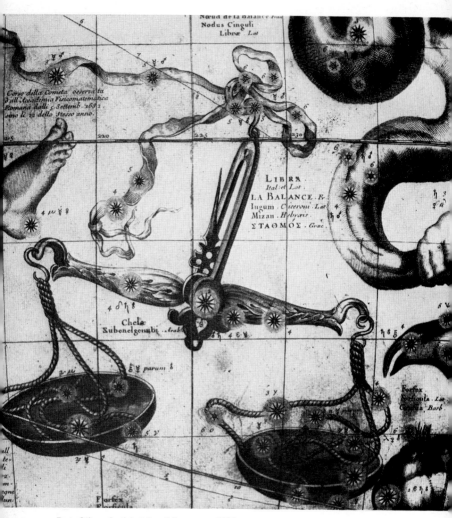

Part of the celestial globe of Deuvez, *c.* 1683

The astrolabe, an ancient sextant, was a tool for measuring celestial angles necessary to both astronomy and navigation. The Baghdad mathematicians in the ninth and tenth centuries could measure angles to within a few seconds on very large instruments.

Wall sundial, dated 1643

The sextant of Al Khujandi had a radius of sixty feet with each minute divided into ten parts.

For the ordinary purposes of daily life it was necessary to divide the day into equal parts. The first tool to do this was the sundial, developed from the shadow stick into a reasonably accurate timekeeper. From early times until the fourteenth century it was customary to divide the period between sunrise and sunset into twelve, a system of variable hours which suited the sundial but was unsuited to consistent measurement.

To the sundial were added sand glasses (still in use as egg-timers), candles and waterclocks. The precise measurement of human time had to wait on the invention of mechanical clocks.

The temple at Karnak: a ceremonial building on a monumental scale

When permanent human settlements began there was also a need to mark out space and define the size of things. Practical geometry to build temples, tombs and palaces, soon developed rules, and standards of measurement. For centuries Egyptian master builders used a unit of length—the cubit—which did not vary more than 1 : 200 from the mean. The royal standard of volume—the apet—was preserved in the Dromus of Anubis at Memphis. At the same period in Mesopotamia a similar standard of length, the cubit, was maintained with almost equal exactitude.

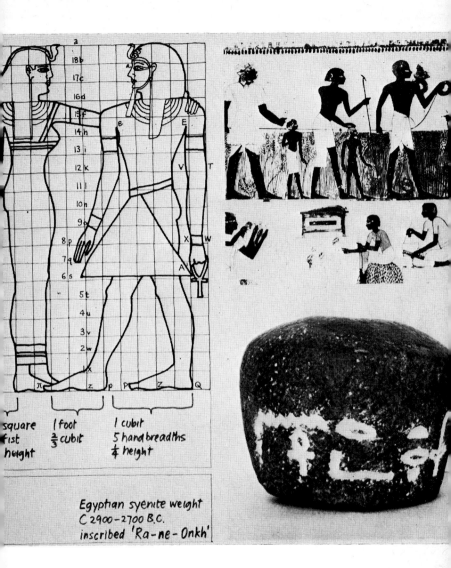

a
18b
17c
16d
15f
14h
13i
12k
11l
10n
9o
8p
7q
6s
5t
4u
3v
2w
1x

e
E
V
T
X W
A

π
z p P Z Q

square
fist
height

1 foot
⅔ cubit

1 cubit
5 handbreadths
4 height

Egyptian syenite weight
C 2900-2700 B.C.
inscribed 'Ra-ne-Onkh'

The Egyptians were skilled in practical measurement. Land surveyors at
work, a stone weight and the formal proportions of ceremonial art

Ancient civil engineers and tax gatherers refined the tools for measurement of length, weight, area and volume, though for many centuries men were content to use the crude anatomical units of length for practical purposes.

All these methods came from practical necessity. It was left to the later civilization of the Greeks, who came first as travellers, then as conquerors, to apply their genius for abstract thought to the empirical methods of earlier men. What to the Egyptians had been merely a post, a stretched string or an area of land became for the Greeks, point, line and plane in a logical exercise which culminated in the thirteen books of Euclid, a monument to reason which stood almost unchallenged for 2000 years.

The first systematic study of logic was also made in Greece, when Aristotle set out his discoveries in logic in a group of treatises known as the 'Organon', in which the beginning of most branches of logic can be found. His theory of the syllogism was an intellectual discovery unequalled in his time, and it dominated logic for 2000 years. Aristotle's syllogism is a way of showing the basic structure of a formal argument, in which a conclusion follows necessarily from previous statements, or premises. The statements have qualifying adjectives like 'all', 'some', 'none'. The four most common statements of this type are:

> All S is P
> No S is P
> Some S is P
> Some S is not P

From which are constructed syllogisms like:

> All books are printed
> All novels are books
> All novels are printed

> Some hair is white
> All dogs have hair
> Some dogs are white

The syllogism is only one of a variety of kinds of inference, and is rarely met in every day speech or thought.

In the fourteenth century, alongside the formal logic of Aristotle and the Mediaeval Schoolmen, there developed a logic of

Head of a Greek statue: symbol of intellectual prowess as well as athletic skill

terms which studied the logical properties of spoken language, and the use of terms like 'or', 'and', if-then' as logical operations. These are the operators of symbolic logic, and the switching circuits of computers, but it was a long time before these exercises in logic could become powerful enough to be used in this way, and much of the history of logic in the intervening time is either trivial or too abstruse to have practical value.

The *Ars Generalis sive Magna* of Ramón Lull, a Spanish religious mystic and poet, was the earliest attempt in formal logic to use geometric diagrams and mechanical demonstrators. With these he sought to convert the infidels to Christianity, and to embrace the whole field of human knowledge.

A Lullian circle is a combinatorial analysis of sets of terms. Given, say, sixteen terms, or their letter symbols representing attributes of the subject, laid around the circumference, and repeated as a concentric circle, all permutations are found by rotating the inner circle. Thus 240 two-term permutations reveal all knowable truths about the subject. Lull believed that every branch of knowledge has a small number of basic principles that must be accepted without question. By exhausting all combinations of those principles we can explore all the knowledge our finite minds can understand. No such primitive truths exist except in the dogma of the constructor, so such 'proofs' as arise are implicit in the choice of 'truths'. The number of circles used varied, mostly only two or three, but his Figura Universalis used fourteen, a staggering complex of possibilities.

Lullian circles, from the *Enciclopedia Universal Illustrada*, Barcelona, 1923

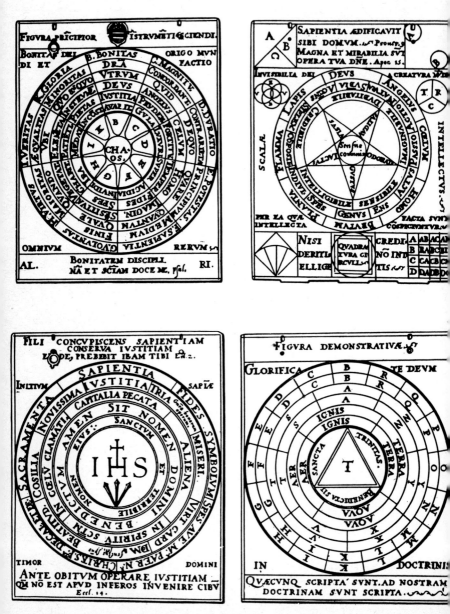

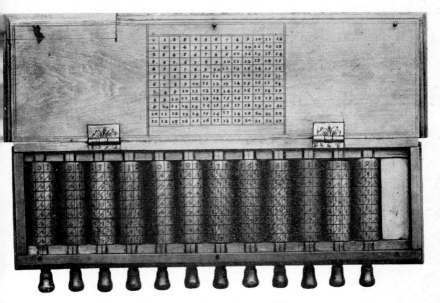

Napier's bones set out on cylinders to form a calculator

◀ Circles used by Renaissance followers of Lull

Although essentially trivial Lull's teachings persisted until the nineteenth century. The machine shown by a Laputian professor to Gulliver in Swift's *Gulliver's Travels* was a satire on Lull's methods, whereby the most ignorant may write books (on any subject) '. . . without the least assistance from genius or study'. But to the philosopher Leibniz, Lull's method was a vision of a universal system of knowledge.

For the diarist Samuel Pepys multiplication and division were a struggle. But before Pepys wrote his diary John Napier had invented a new method. His logarithms substituted simple addition and subtraction for the more difficult processes, and revolutionized manual computing to such an extent that our civilization might not have developed as it did without them. He also devised

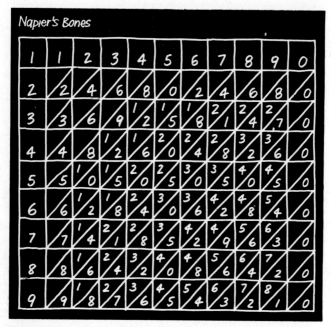

Napier's Bones

1	1	2	3	4	5	6	7	8	9	0

The arrangement of a set of Napier's bones, equivalent to one cylinder of the calculator. Carrying is by adding diagonally, so 3 × 45 = 1(2 + 1)5 or 135

Engraving of John Napier (1550—1617)

Napier's 'bones', or Rhabdology, a quick multiplying device which laid out the multiplication tables 1–9 on strips of paper, wood or bone such that they could be added diagonally. This made automatic carrying possible. Later versions could be rotated so that more complex numbers could be handled.

His logarithms, published in 1614 and calculated by William Briggs to fourteen decimal places by 1624, use the fact that indices of powers of numbers can be added, e.g., $A^5 + A^3 = A^{5+3} = A^8$. A is called the base number, and any number can be represented as a power of A. Common logarithms use a base of 10, so we can multiply and divide any numbers by converting them to powers of 10 and adding or subtracting the indices then converting back. To do this we use tables of logarithms, which are lists of indices, in this case for powers of 10.

The sum $2 \times 3 = X$ becomes:
log 2 0·3010 ($2 = 10^{0·3010}$)
log 3 0·4771 ($3 = 10^{0·4771}$)
$\overline{0·7781}$
But $10^{0·7781} = 6$ so $0·7781 = \log 6$, and the answer is 6.

Pepys solved his problem by buying a slide rule, and found it 'very pretty for all questions of arithmetic'. This now common instrument translates the logarithms of Napier on to sliding or rotating scales, and in so doing becomes an analog computer which substitutes comparisons of length for the numbers being calculated.

Page from an early edition of Napier's logarithms

N		
	9,86278,4220	
4403	3,64374,86854,5953	9,86248,4019
4404	3,64384,73102,9972	9,86014,1825
4405	3,64394,59127,4807	9,85800,6668
4406	3,64404,44928,1475	9,85576,9517
4407	3,64414,30505,0992	9,85353,3381
4408	3,64424,15858,4373	9,85119,8259
4409	3,64434,00988,2632	9,84906,4152
4410	3,64443,85894,6784	9,84683,1057
4411	3,64453,70577,7841	9,84459,8974
4412	3,64463,55037,6815	9,84236,7904
4413	3,64473,39274,4719	9,84013,7845
4414	3,64483,23288,2564	9,83790,8795
4415	3,64493,07079,1359	9,83568,0755
4416	3,64502,90647,1805	9,83345,3724
4417	3,64512,73992,5838	9,83122,7703
4418	3,64522,57115,3541	9,82900,2688
4419	3,64532,40015,6229	9,82677,8680
4420	3,64542,22693,4909	9,82455,5678
4421	3,64552,05149,0587	9,82233,3682
4422	3,64561,87382,4269	9,82011,2691
4423	3,64571,69393,6960	9,81789,2704
4424	3,64581,51182,9664	9,81567,3721
4425	3,64591,32750,3385	9,81345,5740
4426	3,64601,14095,9125	9,81123,8760
4427	3,64610,95219,7885	9,80902,2783
4428	3,64620,76122,0668	9,80680,7802
4429	3,64630,56802,8476	9,80459,3831
4430	3,64640,37262,2307	9,80238,0854
4431	3,64650,17500,3161	9,80016,8876

N		
	9 79133,0937	
4436	3,64599,15374,7712	9,78912,3943
4437	3,64708,94287,1655	9,78691,7943
4438	3,64718,72978,9598	9,78471,2938
4439	3,64728,51450,2536	9,78250,8916
4440	3,64738,29701,1462	9,78030,5906
4441	3,64748,07731,7368	9,77810,3877
4442	3,64757,85542,1245	9,77590,2841
4443	3,64767,63132,4086	9,77370,2796
4444	3,64777,40502,6882	9,77150,3741
4445	3,64787,17653,0623	9,76930,5674
4446	3,64796,94583,6297	9,76710,8596
4447	3,64806,71294,4893	9,76491,2507
4448	3,64816,47785,7400	9,76271,7405
4449	3,64826,24057,4805	9,76052,3288
4450	3,64836,00109,8093	9,75833,0159
4451	3,64845,75942,8252	9,75613,8015
4452	3,64855,51556,6267	9,75394,6855
4453	3,64865,26951,3122	9,75175,6680
4454	3,64875,02126,9802	9,74956,7488
4455	3,64884,77083,7290	9,74737,9277
4456	3,64894,51821,6567	9,74519,2053
4457	3,64904,26340,8617	9,74300,5801
4458	3,64914,00641,4422	9,74082,0539
4459	3,64923,74723,4961	9,73863,6249
4460	3,64933,48587,1249	9,73645,2947
4461	3,64943,22232,4162	9,73427,0610
4462	3,64952,95659,4782	9,73208,9257
4463	3,64962,68868,4053	9,72990,8859
4464	3,64972,41859,2952	9,72772,9434

N		
	9,71902,1679	
4469	3,65021,03546,6036	9,71168,4,7157
4470	3,65030,75231,3196	9,71467,3609
4471	3,65040,46698,6803	9,71250,1034
4472	3,65050,17948,7817	9,71032,9429
4473	3,65059,88981,7266	9,70815,8796
4474	3,65069,59797,6068	9,70598,9132
4475	3,65079,30396,5198	9,70382,0438
4476	3,65089,00778,5638	9,70165,2713
4477	3,65098,70943,8345	9,69948,5957
4478	3,65108,40892,4308	9,69732,0168
4479	3,65118,10624,4470	9,69515,5345
4480	3,65127,80139,9814	9,69299,1490
4481	3,65137,49439,1304	9,69082,8600
4482	3,65147,18521,9904	9,68866,6675
4483	3,65156,87388,6575	9,68650,5714
4484	3,65166,56039,2293	9,68434,5717
4485	3,65176,24473,8016	9,68218,6684
4486	3,65185,92692,4694	9,68002,8613
4487	3,65195,60695,3307	9,67787,1103
4488	3,65205,28482,4810	9,67571,5335
4489	3,65214,96054,0167	9,67356,0167
4490	3,65224,63410,0332	9,67140,5938
4491	3,65234,30550,6278	9,66925,2670
4492	3,65243,97475,8941	9,66710,0360
4493	3,65253,64185,9308	9,66494,9009
4494	3,65263,30680,8310	9,66279,8614
4495	3,65272,96960,6924	9,66064,9176
4496	3,65282,63025,6100	9,65850,0629
4497	3,65292,28875,6724	9,65635,3166

One of the earliest forms of slide rule was a series of circular trigonometric and logarithmic scales known as Oughtred's Circles of Proportion, invented by an English clergyman, William Oughtred, in 1621. In 1632 Elias Allen published Oughtred's book *The Circles of Proportion and the Horizontal Instrument, Both invented and the uses of both written in latine by Mr W. O.* An instrument made by Allen about 1634 combines the circles of proportion with a universal astrolabe and Oughtred's Horizontal Dial, an unusual form of astrolabe.

The mechanical clock, driven by descending weights, developed in the middle ages. When it was invented we do not know, but existing examples date from about 1250. Used in the towers of cathedrals and churches their simple mechanisms soon became elaborated to the greater glory of God and their makers. It was the demand for astronomical instruments and accurate clocks that developed the craft of the clockmaker to the stage where they seemed able to reproduce anything that moved. The age of automata had arrived, and such clocks seemed to seventeenth- and eighteenth-century philosophers a model of the Cosmos, a view which led them to question the presence of God.

Accuracy of timekeeping came with Christiaan Huygens, who applied the principle of the oscillating pendulum to regulate the clock escapement. Early navigators had to stay close to the shore, or steer by familiar stars, for ocean navigation was a chance affair, arduous rather than accurate. With Huygens' clock escapement a new standard of time measurement was possible, for a clock mimics the motions of the heavens in its hands.

William Oughtred's Circles of Proportion

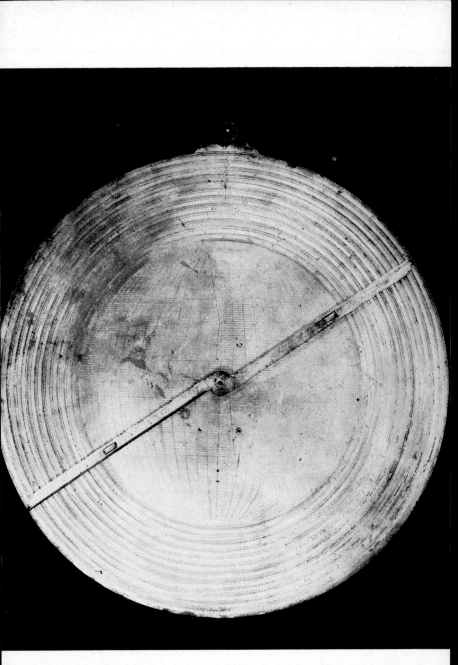

John Harrison (1693–1776) made five chronometers of which this was the first, made in 1735 and tested on a voyage to Lisbon

An early navigator, his instruments and navigation tables

John Harrison's chronometer, in 1735, refined the clock to a precision instrument. Used with accurate tables of longitude and a sextant to fix the angles of the sun or stars, it brought long-range navigation an accuracy which enabled Captain Cook to make his three-year voyage around the world. Harrison's method can be said to precede Watt's governor as a control device, by using the bi-metal strip to compensate for temperature changes which would otherwise make the chronometer go faster in hot weather and slower in cold.

Reference tables have been calculated, published and used

throughout recorded history, from the complex tables of the astronomers to the ordinary multiplication tables and ready reckoner. The burden of calculating, with its dreary repetition, was one of the greatest causes of the effort to devise mechanical calculators. The need to calculate repeatedly and construct tables arose with increasing frequency. One man could spend his life's work on a table, as did William Briggs to calculate Napier's logarithms to fourteen decimal places. These machine-like activities suggested mechanical methods.

The barrier to mechanizing the abacus lay in the clumsiness of the notations used to record its calculations. From the beginning of the Christian era Roman numerals were the most common notation throughout Europe. Try adding MXIX to CIX and the difficulty of devising a machine to do so is apparent. In the tenth century the arrival of the Arabic numerical system, developed by the Moors, opened up the possibility of mechanizing its processes. Significantly Gerbert, later Pope Sylvester II, studied with the Moors and brought back to Europe not only Arabic numerals but also plans for a calculating machine. The Moors had been unable to make it work. Although he spent many years on it, Gerbert was no more successful: his machine was no better than manual calculating. Magnus, another Spaniard, produced a calculator in the form of a brass head with the figures appearing in the mouth. Its practicability and accuracy are not known.

Recently discovered notebooks of Leonardo da Vinci show that he applied his astonishing genius to the design of a mechanical adding machine. Only sketches exist; these illustrate a series of thirteen 10-digit wheels, turned in sequence by a handle. One revolution advanced the first digit wheel for units by one step; after nine steps it returned to zero and passed the action on to the tens wheel, which advanced one step. This is the basic principle of digital counting, adding ones to make any number we can conceive, however large.

Da Vinci's principle lay forgotten in his lost notebooks. It was after almost two centuries that the first practical calculating machines appeared. Another genius reinvented the principle and called it 'Pascaline'. Pascal's first calculating machine, designed in 1642 to assist his tax-collector father, was the beginning of a family of adding machines, the basic principles of which still operate in our desk adding machines.

Gabriel Pascal (1623–62) mathematician and philosopher

Inside of Pascal's calculating machine. The disc rotated by the stylus is under the gears at the top and the results wheels can just be seen at the bottom

Engraving of carrying mechanisms in Pascal's calculating machine, 1642

Pascal's device used a set of wheels, each rotated by a stylus from 0 to 9, transmitting through gears to a set of results wheels from which the answers were read through windows. Up to six figures could be handled, with a fixed decimal point. Tens were carried by a spring ratchet which rose with each unit step up to 9; at 0 it dropped to advance the next result wheel one unit step. Subtraction was performed by adding complements, multiplication by repeated addition.

Pascal could reasonably have expected to make a fortune from so simple and revolutionary a device. Instead it failed but brought

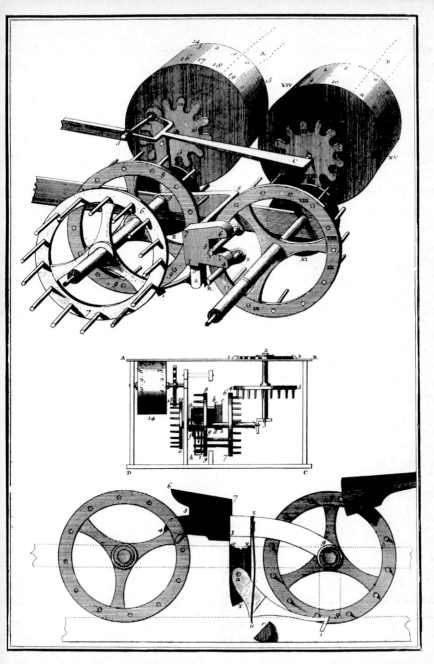

65

Wilhelm Gottfried Leibniz (1646–1716)

Lullian circle of Leibniz representing the totality of the universe

him fame. Businessmen were not impressed, too complicated to repair, too expensive, employing men to do the work would be cheaper, said the employers. Their clerks feared it would lead to unemployment and resisted the machine.

In England Sir Samuel Morland improved on Napier's bones to invent a multiplier, and in 1666 he invented an arithmetical machine which could calculate the four processes of arithmetic.

Gottfried Wilhelm Leibniz was another genius of an age that produced Huygens and Descartes. In the work and philosophy of these men is the beginning of the science of cybernetics. Descartes can be called the father of cybernetics for his study of the human body as a machine, extending the clockwork world of Christiaan Huygens to living organisms. He dreamt of a universal algebra but it was Leibniz, himself a disciple of Huygens, who considered a world of automata after the model of clockwork.

If I were to choose a patron saint for Cybernetics out of the history of science I should have to choose Leibniz. (Norbert Wiener)

Leibniz saw that the mechanical processes of calculation could be paralleled by a mechanization of thought, the reasoning machine. It was around these two concepts that he attempted to build his logical calculus.

Leibniz first brought together calculation and logic in an attempt to construct a universal algebra following the principles of Ramón

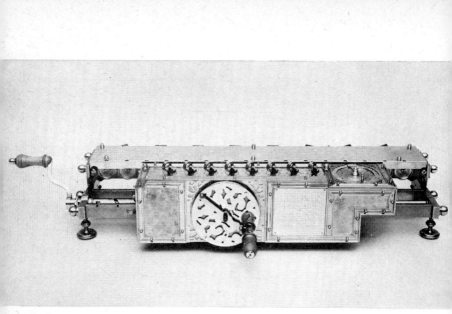

A model of the Leibniz calculator of 1673

Lull. Although more visionary than practicable it foreshadowed the ideas of mathematical notation and symbolic logic. Independently of Sir Isaac Newton he devised methods of differential calculus, and was fascinated by the 'mystic elegance' of binary arithmetic, in which he saw the image of the creation.

Unfortunately he did not see the mathematical application, only a spurious religious use as proof that God could create a universe from nothing, a proof he used to convert the Emperor of China to Christianity, as Lull had sought to convert the infidel with his circles. His association with Huygens aroused an interest in

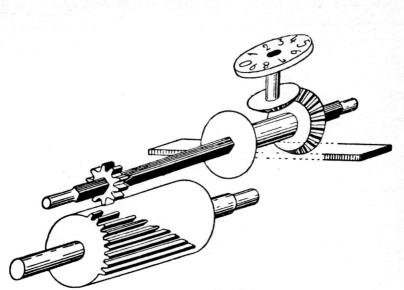

The stepped drum principle invented by Leibniz

mechanical devices. Inspired by the idea of a calculating machine he studied those of Pascal and Moreland. The outcome was a machine which could not only add and subtract but also multiply, divide and extract square roots. His stepped wheel was an advance on Pascal's ratchet, his machine the first general purpose calculator whose principles are still used in modern calculating machines.

Despite improvements in speed, reliability, and convenience, the eighteenth century was not able to provide the technological skill and mechanical precision needed to produce calculators in

De Colmar's commercially successful calculating machine

Charles Thomas de Colmar (1785–1870)

quantity. The first to succeed was Charles Thomas de Colmar, who began selling his calculator to Parisian insurance houses in 1820. Colmar's machine used a Leibniz 'stepped-wheel' in which a drum containing nine teeth, each a different length, turns a small slidable wheel that operates the counters. In 1878 Odhner, a Swedish engineer, patented a 'pin-wheel' method for adding any digit from one to nine.

These basic designs were improved by other inventors using the rapidly growing skills of engineering design. The invention of the typewriter introduced the idea of a keyboard for calculators, which Burroughs achieved in 1892.

All these machines were hand cranked, but a new power source was at hand, electricity, and the development of this kind of digital calculator was complete. Useful as they are their limitations are apparent: a human operator must decide what is to be done, press keys to do it and read out the results. Such machines are far short of the goal of an automatic, self-regulating calculating machine which can take a problem and return a completed answer. To get there two more ingredients are needed, a logical power to take decisions and control operations, and an automatic means of receiving and storing information.

The Logic Demonstrator invented by Charles, third Earl Stanhope, in 1777, was the world's first logic machine. A deceptively simple pocket-size instrument, it could solve traditional syllogisms, numerical problems in logical form, and also elementary questions of probability.

Behold then the luminous perspicuity and most beautiful simplicity of this new form of logic. (Charles, Earl Stanhope)

Stanhope was an eccentric eighteenth-century British statesman and scientist with many inventions to his name, including a calculating machine using geared wheels and an arithmetic machine similar to Pascal's. His Logic Demonstrator used a class logic that interpreted any proposition as an identity. By 'All men are mortal' we mean the class of all men is identical to a portion of the class of all mortal things.

The device is a block of wood with a centre window behind which are two slides, one grey for the first premise and a red glass for the second premise. By sliding first the grey to fill part or all of the window then the red glass to fill part or all of the window, a logical conclusion can be reached from the relationship of red and

Earl Stanhope's Logic Demonstrator, 1777

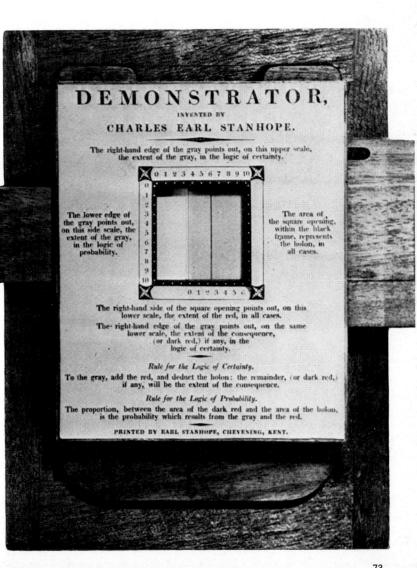

Part of the mechanism of the Stanhope calculator

grey. The task of translating identities is tedious. The horizontal numbers allow numerical deduction to be made, and the vertical scale, using the grey slide from the top, is the probability scale.

By applying ordinary algebra to sets of classes George Boole, an English logician, showed they could be handled in the same way as algebraic symbols or numerical quantities. His Boolean algebra deals with connecting words like 'not', 'and', 'or', as symbols so it can be used to analyse many forms of argument, making it a powerful tool in science and engineering. This first step towards a modern symbolic logic fulfilled Leibniz' dream of a calculus of logic.

The set of all subclasses of a universe class is a Boolean algebra. The number of subclasses depends on the number of

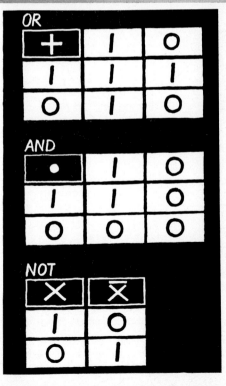

The Stanhope Arithmetical
Machine of 1780

Truth tables for a two-valued
Boolean algebra, which applies
to the binary number system

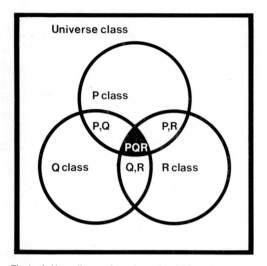

The basic Venn diagram for a three-class logic and the eight regions which make up the universe of discourse

elements in the universe class, and yields different Boolean algebras. For example, a universe class of three elements and eight subclasses related by the operations of addition, multiplication and taking complements, make up a Boolean algebra. The simplest is a two-value algebra having only two elements, the universe class (having only one member) and the empty class.

John Venn and William Jevons devised methods of using Boolean algebra to demonstrate class logic and so helped develop it to its modern form. John Venn's method, known as Venn diagrams, was ingenious : in its basic form three circles are drawn to overlap in all possible ways, dividing the plane, representing a universe of discourse, into eight regions.

William Jevons, whose fame as inventor of a logic machine has obscured his other contributions to logic, economics and philosophy, saw Boole's algebraic logic as the greatest advance since Aristotle. His machine, which used a logical alphabet of four terms, was built in 1869 to perform operations on Boolean principles. It was the first to have the power to solve complicated problems faster than the unaided logician.

Jevons' Logic Machine

Automatic calculation

'One evening I was sitting in the rooms of the Analytical
Society at Cambridge . . . with a table of logarithms lying
open before me. Another member coming into the room, and
seeing me half asleep called out, "Well, Babbage, what are
you dreaming about?" to which I replied, "I am thinking that
all these tables might be calculated by machinery." '
(Charles Babbage)

Charles Babbage is the undisputed source of the automatic
computer. Despite the ultimate failure of his own efforts, he
succeeded in mapping out the principles and operating procedures
which all later digital computers have followed. The recurrent
theme of calculating reference tables appears again as the stimulus
which started Babbage on his dream. In essence it was a practical
one, embarked on in the interest of accuracy and the economy of
labour, he regarded repetitious calculation as 'one of the lowest
occupations of the human intellect'.

Governments and official bodies were responsible for the
preparation of great volumes of complex tables, most of which
needed human drudgery to calculate them. Babbage wrote a paper
on the tendency to make errors, which once made repeat themselves in spite of elaborate checking methods. He had studied
machines by previous inventors and was so impressed by that of
Charles, third Earl Stanhope, that he used it as a starting point for
a machine of his own. He may have known also of a differencing
machine invented by Johann Helfrich von Müller thirty years
earlier, and similar in principle to his own, but if the debt existed it
was never acknowledged. His first Difference Engine was completed in 1822, worked and was used to produce simple tables.
With government funds he began a larger Difference Engine. It was
never completed, but a small portion was put together. Both
machines embodied in wheels, shafts and cranks the principle of
constant differences.

Charles Babbage (1792–1871)

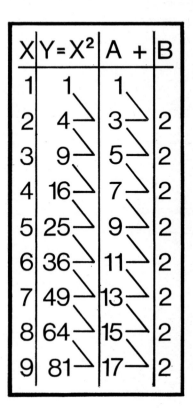

X	Y = X²	A	+	B
1	1	1		
2	4	3		2
3	9	5		2
4	16	7		2
5	25	9		2
6	36	11		2
7	49	13		2
8	64	15		2
9	81	17		2

Sequence of operations
followed to find squares by
the method of differences

The 1822 Engine was a special purpose calculator which solved polynomial equations (which are equations with more than two terms) having up to seven terms. The later Engine would have extended this to twenty places. The basic principle is that at some level the differences are constant between values calculated for a formula. Once the initial entries and the procedure to follow have been set the values can be calculated by addition only. For example, to find the squares of successive integers (1, 2, 3, 4, . . .) the formula is $Y = X^2$, the constant difference is 2, the initial values are $Y = 1$, $A = 1$, $B = 2$, where A is the first difference, B the second difference. The additive sequence $A_1 + B_2 = A_2$, $A_2 + Y_1 = Y_2$ repeats to produce the table of squares.

Replica of the Babbage Analytical Engine. The columns for storage and calculation ('mill') are in the centre; horizontal racks set numbers for the printer, far left

In 1833 Babbage turned his back on the unsuccessful second Difference Engine. Misunderstandings over government backing and that most frequent stumbling block for inventors—a lack of adequate materials and engineering technology—prevented him from carrying out his designs. From then on he worked only in drawings to evolve his grand vision, an entirely original machine to perform any type of digital calculation. The Analytical Engine, as he called it, occupied the rest of his life but was never built, although a model was made from his drawings by his son. It can be seen preserved in London's Science Museum.

Detail of the central columns of the Analytical Engine

The truly automatic calculator could not be made until a mechanical method could be found to give it information and control its operations. The answer was found in a weaving process, developed by several innovators in the eighteenth century, to culminate in a machine, the Jacquard loom, which used a train of punched cards to control the lifting of thread. By this means infinitely variable instructions could be stored, fed to the machine and repeated as necessary. Joseph Marie Jacquard demonstrated

Model of Jacquard apparatus

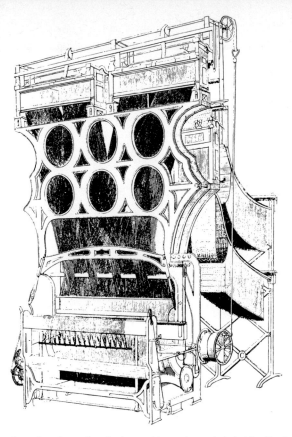

Engraving of an automatic Jacquard loom, demonstrated at the Great Exhibition of 1851

his loom in 1806, by 1812 11,000 had been sold in France and some 1000 more in the rest of Europe.

To weave figured silks a complex combination of different warp threads is lifted at each throw of the shuttle. On the manual drawloom a cord was attached to each thread; for every throw an assistant selected the cords according to a chart and lifted them together. Jacquard substituted punch cards for the manual task of the assistant. Sets of cards, each punched with a pattern of holes, were linked together to pass over a drum. A set of rods, with each rod connected to a group of warp threads, was pressed against each card in sequence. The rods which passed through holes lifted the corresponding threads to form the pattern at each throw.

Henry Babbage, Charles's son, had made a working model of the central portion of his father's Analytical Engine. This view shows the printer and part of the mill

A portrait of Jacquard, woven on one of his own looms, used 24,000 punched cards in the 'program', a weave so fine it was often taken for an engraving. Babbage brought back one of these portraits for Queen Victoria and was familiar with the operation of the loom. He noted that 'the Jacquard loom weaves any design which the mind of man can conceive'.

The Countess of Lovelace, describing the operation of the Analytical Engine, wrote, '. . . [it] weaves Algebraic patterns, just as the Jacquard loom weaves flowers and leaves'. Lady Lovelace played a brief but important part in Babbage's life. A mathematician of genius herself, she mastered Babbage's plans for the Engine, contributed to its development and anticipated many of the ideas and methods used today, including the concept of binary arithmetic, using ones and zeros.

Babbage's automatic computer had a 'mill' or arithmetic unit to do all the operations of arithmetic and put them together in any programmed sequence. Input and program were both done by punched cards on the Jacquard principle, using the punching to represent mathematical symbols. The store could hold 1000

Detail of cams in the mill column. Babbage demanded high
engineering skill to make his intricate drawings reality

fifty-digit numbers, with an auxiliary store of constants (such as
logarithms) and programs. It had a built-in power of judgment to
choose programs. Output was in the form of either punched cards,
direct printing or as type set ready to print. It would have performed one addition per second. Babbage had conceived a
machine able to operate 'in the absence of all necessity for the

Hollerith hand punch

intervention of human intelligence during the performance of its calculations'. As the concept of an automatic universal computer, it anticipated all the basic parts and functions of a modern digital computer in a mechanical form.

By the time Babbage died in 1871 all the ingredients to make the electronic computer had been discovered. In 1835 Roschen-schold published the discovery that an electric current would flow only one way through some solids—the basis of the solid state or semi-conductor diode as a device for controlling electron flow; Boolean algebra awaited application to switching circuits; electricity was becoming readily available as a power source.

Hollerith adding unit

It was electricity that made Babbage's dream reality, in the use of electricity to operate mechanical devices, electromagnetic relays, counters and electric motors. Electric current replaces much machinery, transmits information at high speed and can operate at a distance.

For Dr Herman Hollerith, a statistician with the US census office, census analysis was as laborious as calculating tables. He knew Jacquard's method and applied it to breaking down census replies. The outcome, in 1886, was an electromechanical punched-card system which tabulated the 1890 census of a 65-million population in two and a half years.

Engraving of Hollerith's counting/sorting machine, 1890

To punch, sort and tabulate are the essentials of a data processing system, such as Hollerith devised. His method used 3 × 5-inch cards, with holes punched one at a time as the census form was read, breaking down the census results into either simple yes/no answers, or for more complex questions, coded groups (age-group, occupation) suited to punch-card recording. This was 'read' by a 'pin' press having a pin corresponding to each hole position in the card. The pin above a hole passed through the hole to a mercury-filled cup, so sensing the hole and passing current. The signal was read by an electromagnetic counter, able to count from 1 to 10,000, in a bank of counters. There were 26 positions on the card reserved for sorting, so that one signal would energize an electromagnet to raise the appropriate lid in the sorting box, the operator would then put the card into the box. All other operations were manual. Soon afterwards James Powers designed mechanical equipment for the same purpose, which was used for later census work.

The pin press on a later version of the Hollerith machine

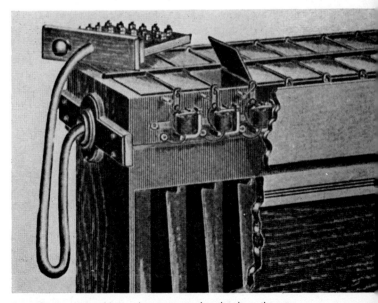

The sorting box, opened by an electromagnet when the pin on the press completed the circuit

Today we use Hollerith methods in data processing systems, and to provide input and storage for electronic computers. Hollerith set up the Tabulating Machine Company, to exploit the commercial value of his machine, applying them not only to the statistical work of censuses but to compiling costs, analysing pay rolls, keeping inventories, insurance analyses, railway operations, accounting—indeed, all the kinds of commercial jobs for which similar machines are used today.

With the exception of the slide rule all the calculating tools so far described have been based on the digital methods of counting. The measurements of the physical world do not easily fit so neat a scheme of units; so for accurate measurement, and the control that would then be possible, other methods were needed that would measure and calculate. The analog process measures variables like length, volume, weight, speed, temperature, which change smoothly and continuously, not in steps.

An example is Kelvin's Tide Predictor, made in 1879, which could predict the times of tides and the height of water around the coast of Britain for any number of years ahead. Because it was an analog any intermediate tide level could be measured. The application to making the tide tables so necessary to coastal navigation is apparent. The inventor William Thompson, Lord Kelvin, was a nineteenth-century scientist who made many contributions to the evolution of cybernetics. He developed the mathematics of thermo-dynamics, giving his name to an absolute scale of temperature. His study of electrical discharge from Leyden jars started Hertz on research into electromagnetic waves, the beginning of radio, and he devised many electrical measuring and recording instruments. His studies of communication theory made possible the first Atlantic submarine cable.

The Tide Predictor was a mechanical system of drums, cable and dials, but it showed that differential equations, which deal with relationships between variables, could be solved by machine.

Kelvin's Tide Predictor

The Differential Analyzer built by Dr Vannevar Bush at MIT, with
integrating units in foreground

In 1923 Wainright developed Kelvin's ideas and in 1925 Dr
Vannevar Bush, at MIT, constructed the first analog computer to
solve differential equations. Called a Differential Analyzer it was
mechanical, apart from electric motors, using differential gears
whose angular rotation indicated quantities. Measuring the angles
limited its precision, although an electrical measuring method was
built into later models.

Analog computers are of great importance when continuous
monitoring and control are needed, but they are usually built for
a specific purpose and so are highly specialized. The general
purpose or universal computer is almost always digital, but can do
the work of an analog computer by using means of converting
measurements into countable quantities.

In the 1930s the theoretical groundwork for the electronic
computer was being laid. Fleming's thermionic valve was already
in use in radio communications, the speed with which it could
switch or change state far exceeded that of any machine or
electro-magnetic relay. Dr Bush encouraged one of his students,
Claude E. Shannon, to write a thesis, later published as 'A Symbolic
Analysis of Relay and Switching Circuits'. In it Shannon was able

to demonstrate the parallel between algebraic logic and switching circuits. Boolean logic had met the electric switch. The binary number system could be represented as true or false values by the open or closed state of electrical circuits. The bit (binary digit) could be used as a universal unit of information. 'A bit is the choice between plus and minus; it is the amount of information needed to remove the uncertainty between yes and no.'

In 1936 an Englishman, A.M.Turing, devised the Turing machine—an abstract general model of all logic machines— using ideas that define the general structure, feasibility and limitations of digital computers. A Turing machine is an imaginary model, a simple machine to do complex calculations step by step. It comprises an infinitely long tape, divided into squares, a box to expose only one square at a time and a set of instructions or program. Only four steps are possible, to move the tape one square to left or right, alter the symbol in the exposed square, or

General arrangement and program for a Turing machine

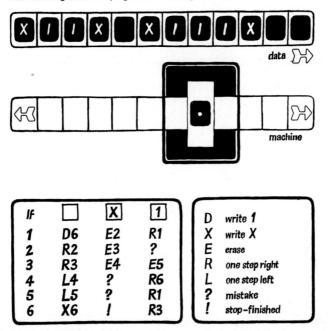

IF	☐	X	1
1	D6	E2	R1
2	R2	E3	?
3	R3	E4	E5
4	L4	?	R6
5	L5	?	R1
6	X6	1	R3

D	write 1
X	write X
E	erase
R	one step right
L	one step left
?	mistake
!	stop–finished

stop. Any square may be blank or contain a symbol. Although not practical calculators these devices give a theoretical measure of optimum performance, against which the performance of actual machines can be assessed.

After the war he began theoretical work for the construction of ACE; the Automatic Calculating Engine, and the Pilot ACE was completed in 1950. It was in some ways ahead of ENIAC, its American counterpart, and was unequalled for some five years.

Turing also considered the use of a computer to help explain human behaviour and the working of the human brain, drawing parallels between the brain and the universal computer. He wrote a paper, 'Can a machine think?', and exchanged ideas with Norbert Wiener, who was at that time crystallizing the ideas that formed the basis of cybernetics.

Before electronics took command the mechanical computer was given one last crucial fling in 1937, when Howard Aiken designed his first machine to solve polynomial equations. With IBM he began a general-purpose machine, the Automatic Sequence-controlled Calculator Mark 1, in 1939. Three years later he read Babbage, felt himself addressed personally from the past, and introduced the Mark 1 manual with this quotation:

If, unwarned by my example, any man shall succeed in constructing an engine embodying in itself the whole of the executive department of mathematical analysis . . . I have no fear of leaving my reputation in his charge, for he alone will be able to appreciate fully the nature of my efforts and the value of their results. (Babbage)

The ASCC was similar to the Analytical Engine, numbers being stored on registers containing sets of wheels. Each wheel carried one decimal digit, 24 to a register (one for the sign) and 72 registers. Each wheel rotated according to its number and was controlled by a telephone relay. Punched paper tape, not cards, carried the instructions and as each step was specified separately, programming was tedious.

The whole machine was electromechanical. Completed in 1944 it was presented to Harvard where it worked for fifteen years. Bernstein, in his book *The Analytical Engine*, describes a visit to the ASCC, 'when it was working, one could go in and listen to the gentle clicking of its relays, which sounded like a room full of ladies knitting'.

Aiken's Automatic Sequence-controlled Calculator, built for IBM and later installed at Harvard

Research into magnetic circuits for telephone relays led to the invention of the binary adder by George R.Stibitz at Bell Telephone Laboratories in 1937, and then to his Complex Number Computer, the first program-controlled electrical digital computer in 1938. In 1940 this machine was demonstrated to the Mathematical Society of Dartmouth College. In the audience were a number of men who were to make contributions to computer development, including Norbert Wiener and John W.Mauchly.

Mauchly, frustrated by the inability to cope with enormous numbers of calculations, began to study how electronic devices could compute at high speeds. Spurred on by Wiener, he went to the Moore School and there met J.Presper Eckert.

Yet again the need to prepare tables, this time missile trajectory tables for the US Armed Forces, acted as the stimulus for improving methods of calculation. Mauchly and Eckert tackled the problem. The result was ENIAC, The Electronic Numerical Integrator and Calculator, the first to use electron flow in thermionic devices to replace mechanical parts. Except for input and output it had no moving parts, all storage, number manipulation and operations control was by electronic circuits.

Designed by Eckert and Mauchly at the Moore School of Electronic Engineering, ENIAC started work in 1945. It contained 18,000 valves, mainly double triodes, consumed 150 kilowatts of electricity and had a pulse speed of 100,000 pulses per second. Its mode of operation was very similar to the ASCC but in electronic terms, using decimal numbers and punched cards for input. Other machines, EDVAC, EDSAC, UNIVAC followed. In 1944 John van Neumann began an association with the Moore group. He proposed the 'stored program' and made many contributions to the development of computers.

Automatic computers are now almost exclusively electronic because they have developed from the same technology as radio and television, radar and radio telescope. But it is possible to build a computer using any device having two alternative states, controllable from one state to another. These could just as well be optical, pneumatic, hydraulic or chemical, all methods now subjects of intensive research.

ENIAC calculating machine. Dr J.Eckert (right) and Captain Goldstine hold a plug-in decade unit

How a computer is organized. Data follows the outer path from input to output, instructions follow the inner path

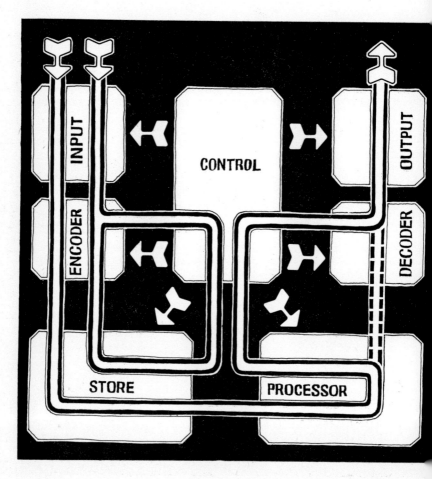

The digital computer

'A child instructed in arithmetic, who has made an addition according to the rules, can feel quite sure that—as far as that sum goes—he has found out everything it lies within the human genius to discover.' (René Descartes)

The digital computer we know today is much more than either the efficient calculating tool sought by Pascal and Liebniz, or the mechanical data processing machine of Hollerith.

The words to 'calculate' and 'compute' are synonymous—meaning 'to determine by calculation, to reckon, to count', but we can distinguish between a calculator and a computer. Babbage's phrase, '[without] necessity for the intervention of human intelligence', implies the difference—calculators are docile machines but the digital computer is capable of selecting alternatives, and so deciding its own course of action.

Because it is a general problem solver, not confined to mathematical uses only, the term computer has been challenged as too limited. The concepts used in the computer are those of the information system and since the messages it handles can have any meaning which we might choose to give them it is a true information machine. Mathematics or music, poetry or payroll, accounts or astronomy, storing information or controlling processes are all one to the messenger electrons of the computer. Being a general-purpose machine, it can switch from one task to another by a change of program.

Computers today are systems which can be put together in various combinations from a range of units. Needs may vary widely: for the scientist fast calculation with only limited storage, for the businessman large capacity file storage and a variety of outputs but simple calculations. Assembling units meet these needs and allow the system to be altered as the need changes. The five main parts of a computer system are: input, store, control, processor and output, the same general arrangement that Babbage gave his Analytical Engine. Separate units, connected by data channels, form two main groups: the 'central processing unit' (CPU) includes control, processing and high speed storage; the

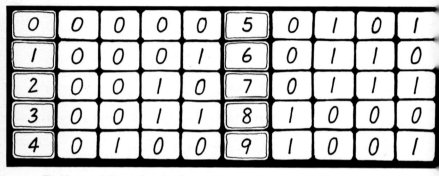

0	0	0	0	0	5	0	1	0	1
1	0	0	0	1	6	0	1	1	0
2	0	0	1	0	7	0	1	1	1
3	0	0	1	1	8	1	0	0	0
4	0	1	0	0	9	1	0	0	1

The binary code for numbers 1 to 9

'peripheral units' are those used for input, output and additional storage. Input and output can be at a distance from the main computer, and are then known as remote terminals. Airlines use them to make reservations from all over the world through one central computer, and through terminals many different people can get answers to different problems from the same computer, methods known as time-sharing and multiprogramming.

A digital computer uses precisely timed pulses, step by step, to operate at very high speeds. The electrical signals, or clock pulses, are 'bits' (binary digits) which travel at the speed of light to carry coded messages which operate the electronic circuits of the computer.

A pulse language for the computer can be represented by two digits: one and zero. The zero means no pulse, so no bit, the one means a pulse and so one bit. This number system gets its name

'Alice couldn't help pointing a finger at Tweedledum, and saying, "First boy!" "No how!" Tweedledum cried briskly . . . "Next boy!" said Alice, passing to Tweedledee, though she felt certain he would only shout "Contrariwise!" and so he did.' *Alice Through the Looking Glass*

from binary (Latin *binarius*, from *bini*, two together) having or consisting of two, giving a numerical system with two as base instead of ten. That information can be conveyed using only two symbols is ancient knowledge, used by primitive tribes before finger counting. Red Indians used long and short smoke signals; native drummers high and low pitch drum beats; Celtic Ogam script had high and low chisel marks along a line. Francis Bacon had a binary cypher, A and B representing the whole alphabet. A switch may be open or closed, a bulb on or off, a magnet polarized.

These simple signals are all a computer needs to work. Many different information codes are used in various parts of a computer, or in different kinds of information handling problems, but most are based on the binary system.

We use other number systems daily and because we are familiar with them they seem simple. Although the decimal or metric

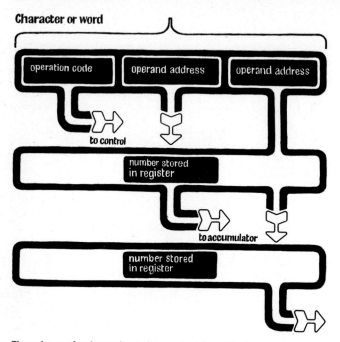

Character or word

| operation code | operand address | operand address |

to control

number stored in register

to accumulator

number stored in register

The make-up of an instruction and the routes followed in the operation

system is widely used for currency, weights and measures, there are still seven days in a week, eight notes in an octave. Why not use a decimal system in computers? We can, but only if the number is first put into binary code, called 'binary coded decimal', which uses four bits to represent each number. Since a ten-base system needs ten symbols, 0 to 9, instead of two, more pulses are needed to represent symbols so any advantage is lost. Nevertheless, codes based on this principle are used when they help the user to communicate with the machine or get information from it.

Information given to a computer must be converted to a language it can use, called a machine language, in which bits combine to form 'words', trains of electric pulses. Combinations can stand for the alphabet, symbols, punctuation, as well as numbers, in data, depending on the code. A machine language or code is a sequence of signals which can be directly interpreted by the control devices of a computer.

The sequence of bits may convey different information if interpreted in different ways. The digits 251271 can be a number—

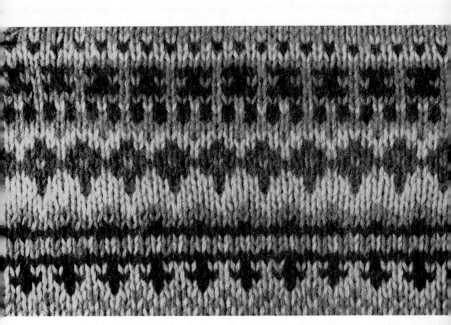

A knitted pattern produced by following a program of instructions

251,271 ; or Christmas Day 1971—25.12.71 ; or an instruction—
do operation 25 to numbers in accumulator 12 and store in
register 71, as instructions are coded in machine language,
divided into operations codes, like 'add', 'store', and addresses to
find stored data.

Using words of standard length the machine language inter-
prets each as a number, statement or instruction, according to the
program. As this language is very different from the ones we use
our problems must first be stated in a language the machine can
translate. The translation program is called a compiler, acting like
a foreman relaying detailed instructions from his boss's orders.

The familiar abbreviations of a knitting pattern, 'Kl, Sl.1, psso.,
K to last 3 sts., K2 tog., Kl.' are instructions from a program every
bit as complex as some computer programs. Like them it is in a
programming language, communicating an organized sequence of
instructions. Programmers writing such a program analyse each
step to be taken, using a 'language' which the machine can
accept.

Programming of early computers was laborious, each step had to be written out separately, often in binary code. Now special programs are stored in the computer which will translate statements in our language into computer terms. This algorithm, or set of instructions, is first written as a source program, in common human language, and as a flow diagram of the sequence. These are then converted to an object program, which puts them in a form the computer can translate.

FORTRAN, for example, derived from 'Formula Translation' is based on algebra plus a few rules of computer grammar, and was devised primarily for scientists and engineers familiar with mathematics. The businessman needs a different language, like COBOL (Common Business Oriented Language), which expresses business problems in a language derived from business English.

Now that scientific and business uses have become inextricably mixed, and one computer may be doing both at the same time, new general-purpose languages have been developed, such as PL/1, which reduces greatly the amount of programming needed. Today, whether you type, draw or speak to a computer to command it or ask a question, the answer can be an immediate response in the same form.

Instruction sequences used frequently become sub-routines, stored in the machine as permanent short programs for use when they occur in the program being run. Since the same program can be used repeatedly with different data, libraries of programs are available to users with similar problems. The written program, fed to the machine, becomes a stored program. One machine can use several stored programs to switch jobs without stopping, a method known as multiprogramming.

Given a program of instructions, and the information to which the program is to be applied, the computer must go through a sequence of operations to produce a result. This it does by applying the rules of Boolean algebra in logic circuits. Logic elements are the building blocks of computer circuits. A machine's properties are largely determined by the way they interconnect. Boolean algebra uses the binary code to represent a true or false condition, with the three operations 'and', 'or' and 'not' each having a corresponding switching or logic element. These are called gates, simple gates have one or two inputs to produce one

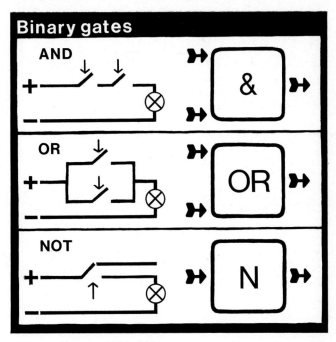

Binary gates

AND

OR

NOT

The three basic gates of logic circuits

output. An electric light bulb, some switches and a battery can be wired up to show how each of the three operations is done by a different kind of gate.

The 'and' gate has two switches wired in series, that is one after the other, so that both must be on to give a light. So the 'and' gate has output 1 only if both inputs are 1, the logical equivalent of multiplication.

Similarly the 'or' gate has two switches, but now in parallel, side by side, so that if either is on the bulb will light. The 'or' gate has output 1 if either or both inputs are 1.

The 'not' gate behaves like a wrongly connected switch that reads 'on' when the light is off and vice versa, so it has an output 1 for input 0 and output 0 for input 1. It represents Boole's idea of logical negation and is used in computer circuits to invert the logic.

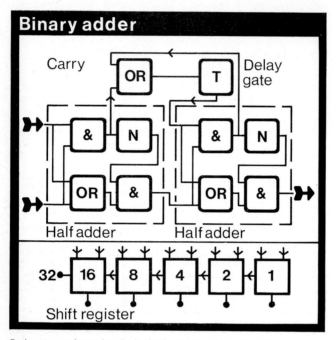

Binary adder

Carry

OR — T — Delay gate

& — N — & — N

OR — & — OR — &

Half adder — Half adder

32 ● 16 ← 8 ← 4 ← 2 ← 1

Shift register

Basic gates used to make a logic circuit, a binary adder, consisting of two half-adders linked by a delay gate which holds the carry digit for one pulse. A shift register is essentially a string of adders

All these operations can be shown in truth tables which make it possible to analyse complex logic circuits without having to build them. In the complex paths of integrated circuit assemblies we no longer know the precise paths a signal may follow. The same operation may be done several times simultaneously and the circuit checks itself to eliminate faulty paths.

Combinations of simple gates are used to make binary half-adders and adders. The half-adder can add two digits together but has no means of carrying a digit forward to the next place. With a second half-adder included the circuit becomes an adder able to carry automatically from column to column. All computer arithmetic is done by repeated addition, or taking complements for subtraction and division.

Half-adders can be used to compare numbers by subtraction, so directing the computer to take alternative actions, which are different for a positive number, a negative number or zero. Comparison by subtraction is the computer's decision-making ability, a choice between alternatives. But the computer cannot find the alternatives—these must be determined by the human analysis of the problem and given to the computer to calculate the probabilities and compare them.

Punch operator keying in data on to punch cards

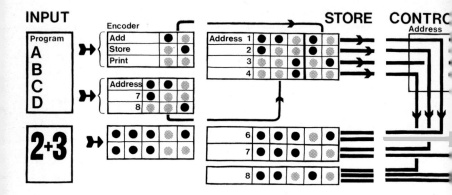

To complete a calculation the program instructions are:

A Go to address 6, take number to accumulator
B Go to address 7, take number to accumulator
C Take number from adder and store in address 8
D Go to address 8, take number to printer

By following a simple calculation through the computer we can see the functions of the five parts: input, store, control, processor, output:

1 A computer carries out a simple task by adding together two numbers, 2 + 3. The written program and number data are fed in by an input unit, converted to binary code by an encoder, using a five-bit word, then sent to their storage addresses. Each instruction has a three-bit address code, plus a two-bit operational code—'add', 'store', 'print'. The operations code is used to direct each number along its correct channel from the control, and the address code to select the next number from the store, or to return a number to the store.

2 The store holds each word in two separate registers from which each bit can be read in turn. From address 1 the instruction goes to the control unit, which reads the operations code and address code, holds the operations code and sends it to address 6 for the first number. The operations code 'add' directs the number 2 to the accumulator (a temporary store) in the processor, where it is placed ready to be added to the next number when it comes.

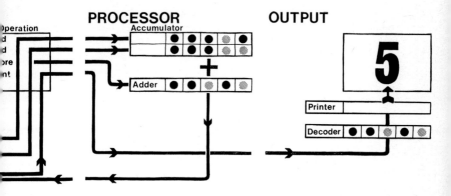

PROCESSOR

Accumulator

Adder

OUTPUT

5

Printer

Decoder

Operation
d
d
ore
nt

3 The control, following instructions as before, fetches the next number, 3, from address 7 in the same way. When the accumulator receives it the two numbers are immediately added to produce a new binary number. The processor, having calculated the result, must be cleared ready for a new calculation, so step 3 tells the control to send the result to address 8. The number could stay there but step 4 brings it out again and instructs control to 'print', so the number is sent to the printer.

4 Addresses 6, 7 and 8 are now cleared, that is put into a state of zero or blank, ready for new numbers. If new numbers are read in and steps 1–4 repeated a new result can be produced. For example, an extension of the program to read the number in address 7 to address 6, and that in address 8 to address 7, would construct the Fibonacci series 2, 3, 5, 8, 13, 21. The next number, 33, needs six bits so the calculation must end, but an actual store can take much larger numbers by dividing them between several registers.

5 The signal sent to the decoder is converted from the binary number 00101 to the decimal digit 5 and printed to give an output. Despite the number of steps, each taking five bits through the machine, the time taken would be very short indeed, only a few millionths of a second.

In computer installations there are many different ways and different pieces of equipment for doing each of these jobs. Input is any means of giving data to the system, and many of these are also ways of storing data away from the computer. Punched cards are still an important way of handling information. Direct descendants of Jacquard and Hollerith, they are now about the size of a dollar bill and have 80 columns or more for punching. The machines that handle them are also derived from Hollerith's and Powers' machines—the key punch, the verifier for checking previously punched cards, the card reader which converts the code recorded by holes into electrical impulses, and the sorter which senses the holes and puts the cards in any order asked for by the operator.

Similar to punched cards is papertape, which also uses punched holes, usually round, but on a continuous roll of paper, which again can be read to convert holes to electric impulses.

Printed documents can be read by optical scanners, although reading handwriting is not practical as yet. Magnetic characters, familiar in the E13B characters on cheques, contain magnetic particles that can be sensed by a magnetic scanner.

The light pen on a visual display screen, the typewriter (or keyboard) and now the human voice are means by which a human being can communicate directly with the computer. Computers themselves can communicate with and give input to other computers. Distance is no obstacle to most of these methods of input, as data links can be used along the normal telephone system.

Magnetic tape and magnetic discs are methods of storage which provide input at high speed. Magnetic tape is a plastic ribbon coated with a ferrous oxide which can be magnetized to form binary bits of information, packed closely together and read at a rate of several hundred thousand bits per second. Like ordinary recording tape it can be stored indefinitely and erased for re-recording. The one disadvantage is that it is a tape, so to get information near the end of it the whole tape must go through the machine.

A solution to this drawback is disc storage, resembling a stack of records rotating at high speed, and read by magnetic heads which move in and out between discs. This is random access as any address can be found on demand without having to go through the whole disc. A similar method is used to store information magnetically on the surface of a drum.

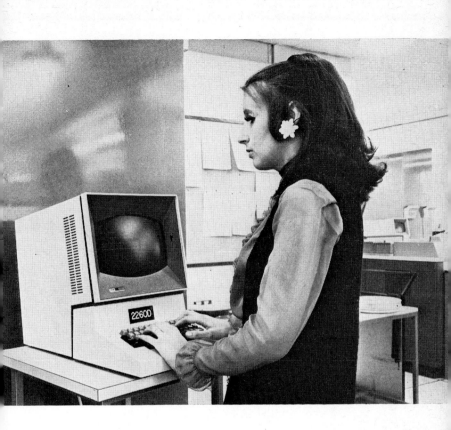

Visual display terminal: the operator keys in information, which appears on the screen, and reads the reply on the screen

Inside the computer, however, all these ways of storage are far too slow for the processing speeds of the control and processing units, where things happen in nanoseconds (one thousand millionth of a second). Here different methods are called for and ever faster types of storage are being sought after. The most common today is magnetic core storage, in which minute ring magnets a few hundredths of an inch in diameter are threaded on to wires which can carry electric signals. Currents of electricity

Core plane showing ring magnets strung on to crossed wires

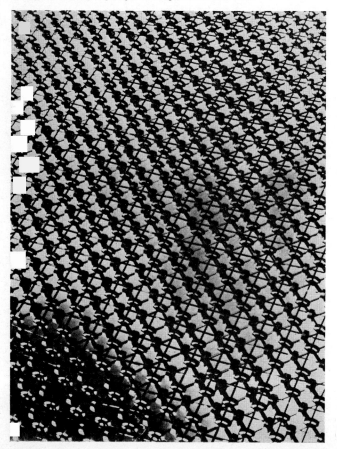

Control panel on the central processing unit of a computer system, the IBM system/360

through the wires magnetize the cores in one of two directions so that polarity represents one and zero of binary. A sensing wire detects the polarity of a particular core to read data, which must be immediately written back again if the information is to be retained.

The central processing unit (CPU) houses the control unit and the processor or arithmetic/logic unit. The control unit is the centre directing the flow of electronic traffic throughout the system, regulating and deciding courses of action according to the program of operating instructions. It selects input and output units, allows the operator to alter the program, interrupt it or get progress reports at any time during operation.

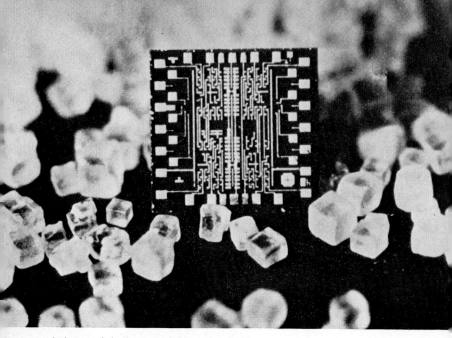

An integrated circuit. surrounded by grains of salt

The arithmetic/logic unit does all calculations and decision-making using the logic elements we examined earlier, assembled into logic modules. In the logic modules are minute transistors, used as switches, diodes and resistors. These modules have shrunk dramatically in size, from the introduction of transistors in 1948 to replace valves, to microminiaturization of integrated circuits. Reducing by a factor of 10 every five years, circuits are now almost 100,000 times smaller.

Now a 'chip' measuring only 0·11 × 0·14 inches can contain 1244 transistors, 1170 resistors and 71 diodes, and even more compression is forecast so that in a decade or so electronic components may be near to a quarter of the density of nerve cells in the human brain.

Although electric pulses travel at the speed of light (186,000 miles per second), the very short operating times of the computer bring even this speed down to a measurable size, to about one foot in a nanosecond, a speed limit which could cause traffic congestion if all the routes in a computer were not as short as possible.

This fact and the microminiature components have tended to make computers smaller, or more powerful for their size.

Calculation time may not be important in ordinary calculations, but many computer applications today must be in 'real time', each taking place as they arise and producing immediate results. This is particularly so for control situations in automation or the regulation of continuous processes where the machine's reaction to complex variable data must at least be as effective as that of the human controller.

The output typewriter of a small computer system, IBM system/3

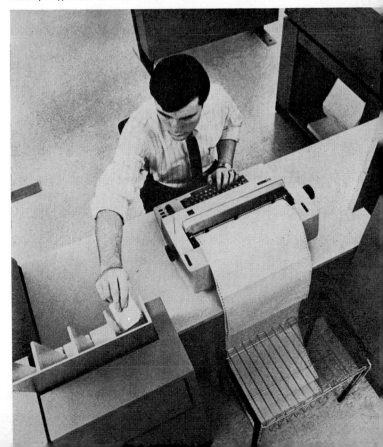

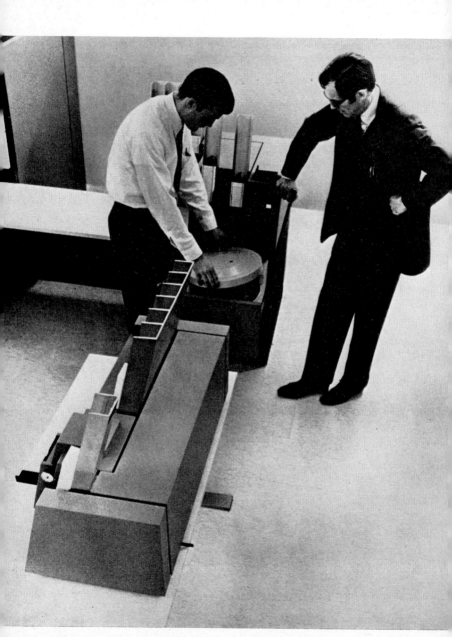

From the central processing unit the result is put back into store to be read out to a decoder, which translates the machine language for the output units. These may print, type, record on tape, display on a screen or tell another computer the answers resulting from the input, using terminals which are the same as or similar to those for input.

The characteristics of a computer system can be summarized as : high calculating speed, ability to retain vast amounts of information, ability to make decisions, and ability to do the first and last of these in real time. The first two are necessary to an information handling system, the latter two typical of a control system which can be applied to many different problems in cybernetics.

Disc storage file in a drawer unit on the IBM system/3

Cybernetics

William Blake's painting of Isaac Newton

'Machines made by the hand of God are incomparably
better ordered and have in themselves more admirable
movements than any that can be invented by the mind of
man.' (René Descartes)

From the temple statues of Antium to the mechanical toys of
Vaucanson early automata, 'robots' of fiction and fact, were but
ingenious mechanisms designed to awe, to amuse, and to advance
scientific knowledge. Behind their persistent fascination lay the
quest for technical skill, to simulate human performance, as well
as the Promethean desire to make the image of man.

In Antium, birthplace of Nero, there were said to be statues that
walked from place to place, and Pindar speaks of animated
images in Rhodes and Crete which 'stand adorning every public
street and seem to breathe in stone, or move their marble feet'.

In seventeenth- and eighteenth-century France were made the
mechanical toys which became the prototype machines of the

Aztec figure with articulated limbs, from Teotihuacan near Mexico City

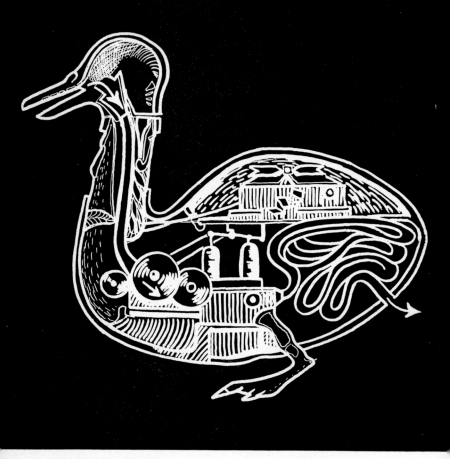

A diagram of the inside of Vaucanson's duck: mechanisms imitating the functions of the living animal

industrial revolution. Jacques de Vaucanson (1708–1782) was the most ingenious maker of all. His duck was made to simulate all the functions of eating, drinking and digesting. It took grain, swallowed it, drank, paddled and quacked. Having digested it then evacuated the remains ! His secret ambition is said to have been to make an artificial man. Bizarre though these automata often were they are a measure of the technical skill which developed and of the attempts made to understand human functions in terms of

Therephim Hebraeorum from *Oedipus Aegyptiacus* by Athanasius Kircher. Mummified heads and oracular figures which 'speak' are referred to in the Bible as Theraphim.

mechanisms. But such artifacts were rarely self-regulating, they repeated a given set of actions without change.

In the first chapter of this book the difference between reflex and conscious action was noted. Before Descartes' time the notion of automatic action was untenable, conscious thought must control human actions. In the early seventeenth century, with the marvellous mechanisms of the clockwork toymakers before him, Descartes could compare their actions with those of the human

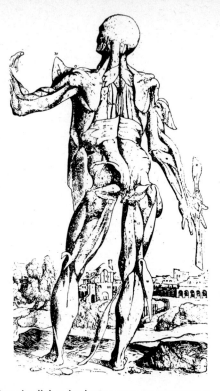

Dissection of the human muscles, by Andreas Vesalius of Brussels. Vesalius ranks with Hippocrates, Galen, Harvey and Lister among the great physicians and discoverers in the history of medicine

body and conclude that the living body too was an automaton obeying fixed rules. From Harvey's discovery of the circulation of the blood he concluded that a hydraulic animal could be built. Because man has a soul, unlike animals in his view, and complex organs for reasoning and speech, the equivalent artificial man could not be made. In his *Discourse on Method* he states the case for this view: 'It is morally impossible that there should be sufficient diversity in any machine to allow it to act in all the events of life in the same way as our reason causes us to act.' Although automata and toys continued to be made, the study of animals in terms of machines gave way to the idea of the machine as a means of converting energy into useful work, an essential prerequisite of the industrial revolution.

The power sources of the industrial revolution, windmill and steam engine, were fore-runners of the science of cybernetics. The windmill cap turned to keep the sails in the eye of the wind for full power, guided by a fantail. To maintain full power and the correct rotation the mill sails must always face full into the wind.

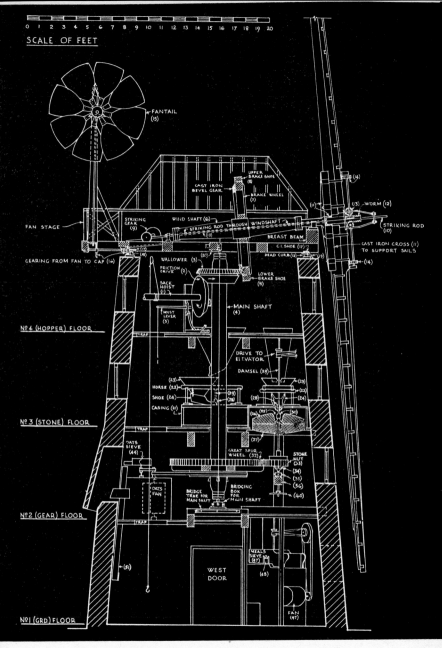

SCALE OF FEET

0 1 2 3 4 5 6 7 8 9 10 11 12 13 14 15 16 17 18 19 20

FANTAIL (15)

FAN STAGE

STRIKING GEAR (9)

WIND SHAFT (6)

STRIKING ROD THROUGH WINDSHAFT

CAST IRON BEVEL GEAR

BRAKE WHEEL (7)

UPPER BRAKE SHOE (8)

WORM (12)

STRIKING ROD (10)

CAST IRON CROSS (11) TO SUPPORT SAILS

BREAST BEAM

C.I. SHOE (17)

DEAD CURB (18)

GEARING FROM FAN TO CAP (14)

WALLOWER (3)

FRICTION DRIVE (2)

SACK HOIST (1)

HOIST LEVER (5)

MAIN SHAFT (4)

LOWER BRAKE SHOE (8)

DRIVE TO ELEVATOR

DAMSEL (29)

Nº 4 (HOPPER) FLOOR

TRAP

HORSE (22)

SHOE (24)

CASING (31)

Nº 3 (STONE) FLOOR

TRAP

OATS SIEVE (44)

GREAT SPUR WHEEL (32)

STONE NUT (33)

(34)

(35)

(36)

(40)

(27)

OATS FAN

BRIDGE TREE FOR MAIN SHAFT

BRIDGING BOX FOR MAIN SHAFT

Nº 2 (GEAR) FLOOR

TRAP

(51)

WEST DOOR

MEALS SIEVE (47)

(48)

FAN (47)

Nº 1 (GRD) FLOOR

Mill cap and fantail forming the wind sensing system of a windmill.
Ballycopeland Mill, County Down, Northern Ireland, *c.* 1784

To do this a fantail with blades was fixed to the rear of the cap. If the wind veered the fantail revolved and through a series of gears caused the mill cap to rotate until the sails were back in the wind. This process was fully automatic and continuous, on a gusty day the cap would continually change position. Inside there was often a simple governor to regulate the distance between mill stones.

In 1788 James Watt applied the governor to his rotative steam engine to regulate its speed, so designing the first servomechanism in engineering practice. His centrifugal pendulum governor was driven from the engine shaft. Ball weights, moving outwards under centrifugal force, were linked to a butterfly valve. As they rose the valve closed, reducing steam and slowing the engine. This lowered the weights so opening the valve again. By adjusting the linkage for a predetermined speed the governor could be made to hold the engine at that speed. Any variation in load, which would tend to vary the speed, was compensated for by the governor. Samuel Butler's Erewhonian professor saw the implication of this application of feedback:

Let one examine the wonderful self-regulating and self-adjusting contrivances which are now incorporated with the vapour engine. Let him watch the way in which, by the governor, it regulates its application of its own strength . . . let him see how these improvements are being selected for perpetuity which contain provision against the emergencies which may arise to harass the machine.

Both devices use negative feedback by acting to oppose variations from a set condition.

Of significance also is the small power of the governor and fantail relative to the engine and wind power they control. This is typical of servosystems which use weak or inefficient signals (the information system) to regulate high power (the corresponding energy system).

This power amplification becomes important when we consider the second element of Wiener's definition, communication.

Bonfires and semaphore served to warn of approaching armadas, the horseride from Ghent to Aix served to get the news through, but expanding empires and rapidly changing economies needed faster methods of transmitting more accurate information. Telegraph, telephone and radio reveal the ways in which electricity met this need. Wires could carry weak signals over long

The ball or centrifugal pendulum governor (right) on James Watt's rotative
steam engine, *c.* 1788

distances at the speed of light, to be amplified at their destination. Later the wireless telegraph performed the same function using electromagnetic waves, applying the principles of Maxwell and Hertz.

It was probably a coincidence that Clerk Maxwell played an important part in the rise of both control and communication. His paper on the governor, published in the Proceedings of the Royal Society in 1868, was the first systematic study of feedback. Wiener and Rosenbleuth chose 'cybernetics', to name their new science, from the Greek word *kubernetes* meaning 'to govern', in recognition of Maxwell's paper. In communications, Maxwell's theory of electromagnetic waves led to the development of wireless telegraphy, radio and electronic methods of radiating signals. This process radiates weak signals having only a small fraction of power applied to produce them, the content of the signal being more important that the efficiency of the system, and uses power amplifiers at the receiving end to boost the signal back to the required level.

The concept of a broadly applied science of control gained further support from the investigations of physiologists. The study of the brain and the nervous system had taken up where Descartes left off, but following different paths. For the physiologists the idea of negative feedback was embodied in Cannon's concept of homeostasis. The body of both man and animal acts as a complex set of regulators for such body conditions as temperature, heart beat, sugar level, and in relation to its outside environment. These systems do not act independently but under control of the central nervous system, to aim towards optimum conditions for the survival of individual and species.

Information theory, communications theory and computer concepts had all been developed in the twenties and thirties. When in 1938 Wiener and Rosenbleuth decided to explore 'the no-man's-land between the various fields of science' their activities attracted scientists with a wide range of interests. This spirit of generalization distinguishes cybernetics from other branches of science. At the Macey Foundation conferences from 1942 to 1953 the application of cybernetics in many fields was developed and the common ground established between communications engineer and neurologist, servo engineer and physiologist, psychologist and biologist.

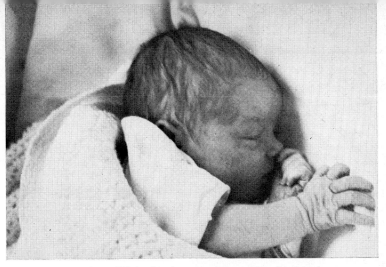

A ten-hour-old baby, for whom the whole world is a 'black box'

The computer, in one form or another, is of great importance to cybernetics. Not only is it able to solve mathematical problems or sort and classify information, it can also make predictions and take decisions based on induction from information. It is at the same time a cybernetic system in itself, the control function of larger systems, and able to become the model of other cybernetic systems.

The technology of both developed in the work of the same group of men. With the common ground between sciences realized, they could be applied to problems in many fields. Ideas familiar to systems engineers could describe processes in muscles and nervous systems, the known organization of animal systems in turn guided the design of communication and control systems.

But cybernetics is not only a scientific tool, for each one of us it is an essential part of life, of the way we live it and the way the world in which we live behaves. Cybernetics is a way of finding out how things behave, not in moral terms but in their actual reactions to events around them.

This pattern of behaviour is complex—we all make decisions and take actions that need great expertise in our daily lives. At the same time the thunder that rolls overhead in a storm is part of the behaviour pattern of a vast system of air pressures and densities, temperature changes, humidity and electrical charges in the atmosphere about us. Apparently random unrelated events, over which we seem to have no control, can be understood in terms of cybernetics.

A baby exploring a new and unknown world has to interpret what his senses tell him. To begin with he has no memory with which to make comparisons, his world is a black box about which

The beginning of exploration, extending the world outside

The first great achievement, walking, opens up a vast new world to explore and new sensations to understand

Putting together sounds and then symbols, speech and reading, is the key to communication and the interchange of ideas

he is completely uncertain, only trial and error experiments can give meaning to a meaningless continuum of light, dark, sound and touch. The basic need is for self-preservation, survival in an uncertain, and therefore hostile, environment. By testing, remembering and comparing, the baby can separate hostile from friendly, nasty from nice, most other humans from mother.

Comparison is fundamental to finding the patterns by which we understand things outside ourselves, and measurement is at the centre of comparison, either as physical measurement or as a judgment of quality. Shape, size, colour, surface, hardness, taste—all can be compared by trial and error, and a baby will make many mistakes, often painful, before it can distinguish say an apple from a ball. Shape, size, colour, even surface and hardness may not be significantly different, but the biting test will decide, and the lesson once learned need not be repeated.

Associations and actions learned in childhood can last throughout life. We speak of 'getting into good habits' or 'bad habits' to describe the acquisition of behaviour patterns.

The baby reaches an age when he needs to explore a larger environment, which is otherwise out of reach, by moving. To do this he must learn to control his movements in order to remain stable, a continuous dynamic process needing judgments of distance, speed, angle and balance, as well as an ability to predict the effect of making any movement.

To complete the baby's efforts to come to grips with his world he must learn to become part of an information system, using a variety of sounds in combination, a coded language of 36 symbols (alphabet and numbers) and a programming language of grammar, to communicate his experiences to the outside world and receive back knowledge from others. He is now able to become part of the information system we call a community and will spend the rest of his life regulating relationships to it.

From this brief view of a baby's development we can draw some conclusions about cybernetics. The distinguishing feature of cybernetics is purpose, the ability to aim towards and achieve a goal. When conditions change there is either a change of goal, or a change of action to remain stable. Adaptation is the change of program to remain stable and is the process of learning, and of teaching. There is also a need to predict the effect of change, a typically human characteristic, or to search randomly the results of possible courses of action to find one which will produce the desired result, which then becomes a learned action.

Learning is itself a dynamic situation which can be used by machines to teach human beings. Teaching machines, to which the pupil reacts by choosing a course of action, interact with the pupil so that both are adaptive control systems. The student uses the machine as part of his brain in acquiring control over some skill. Any skill which can be broken down into steps of increasing difficulty can be taught in this way. The machine presents a problem, gauges the student's response to it and reacts accordingly, passing to more difficult steps as the student's response matches the goal set by the machine. Skills taught in this way are practical, they assume a set body of knowledge, not creative in the sense that a dialogue between a human teacher and his pupil may inspire new knowledge or a creative act.

If machines can teach, can they also be made to learn? Much research has gone into machines which can be made to learn from the results of their actions, a trial and error process imitating that of the baby. While Vaucanson might have envied these attempts to imitate some of the essential functions of the human brain and living creatures, exaggerated claims have sometimes been made for machines which more closely resemble scientific toys.

Maze learning machines have been made to find their way through a maze by trial and error, to memorize the route so that no further trial and error was needed, and to repeat the course. Ross and Wallace both built tracked layouts. Shannon built one that was not restricted to tracks, but instead used a contact finger to sense the walls and make further attempts.

Imitating insects has been tried by a number of experimenters. Insects react by reflex action to certain stimuli, processes known as tropisms (turning) or taxis (movement) of the body. Phototropism is a turning towards light, or light seeking, an action which can be triggered by photoelectric cells in machines.

Dr Grey Walter has made a number of machines with simple animal characteristics—'Nerissa' (Nerve Excitation Inhibition and Synoptic Analogue), 'Cora' (Conditioned Reflex Analogue), and a well-known electronic tortoise called 'Elmer'. This used phototropism and mechanical contact by its 'shell' to hunt along paths resulting from sensing light intensities and obstacles.

Dr Ross Ashby used magnets and electric circuits to make a simple machine he called a Homeostat, since its purpose was to illustrate the process of homeostasis in animals. This machine did not attempt to imitate the form of an animal, and many other experimenters have used analog computers or probability computers to control animal or brain imitating devices.

Uttley's theory of induction of self-teaching machines generated a whole series of projects and models from Uttley, George, Pask, Beer and others. Mackay has designed a machine capable of forming new concepts, but it still seems unlikely that machines can reproduce all the actions of human senses, learning and thought.

The problem becomes apparent when we look at the human nervous system, the most complex structure known to us. Cybernetics came from efforts to unravel its functions, and it continues to explore them. The neurologist studies a communication and control process which enables the millions of cells in the human body to act together as a community, a single organism. The resemblance between the network of the nervous system and the electrical network evolved from communications and information theory was sufficient to prompt their study in each others terms. McCulloch, Wiener, John von Neumann, Lorento No and others had done the ground work and Ross Ashby published his *Design for a Brain* as early as 1931. The sending of messages from receptor to the central nervous system and back is partly electrical, partly chemical. The neurons, of which there are some 10,000 million, are connected by axons, or nerve fibres, to the sensors and muscles of the body. They are also interconnected by dendrites to other neurons in apparent chaos. These connexions are synapses which release a transmitter substance when an impulse is received. This travels across a gap to cause an impulse in the next neuron. Since there are at least 500,000 million synapses the possible combinations and permutations of impulses in the network are immense. The cerebral cortex is organized in specific areas, which correspond to parts of the body. It is characteristic of the brain that there is enormous redundancy since its actions do not depend on individual neurons but on the cumulative action of large numbers of neurons.

Nerve fibres exist in great quantities in all living creatures. Each fibre is a single cell stretched out in a long thin line, which in large mammals and man can be several feet long, but very small in thickness—a kind of living wire. Remote parts of the body are connected by bunches of nerve fibres to the spinal chord, itself made of nerve fibres along the length of the spine to the brain. Signals leaving a sensor, or nerve-ending, travel along the fibre in trains of short electrical pulses, their frequency represents the intensity of the sensation. The fibre acts as a kind of electro-chemical touch paper which when lit sets a sequence of actions in

The brain controls the physical actions of the body through the nervous system, and chemical action via the pituitary gland and endocrine systems

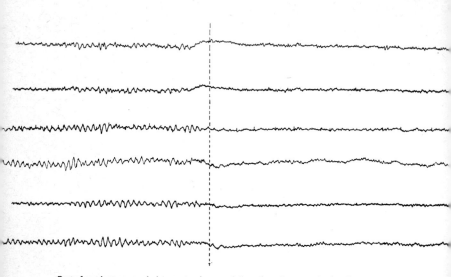

Part of an electroencephalogram tracing: each line of tracing records signals from one electrode attached to the head. The dotted line marks the change of activity from eyes open to eyes closed

motion. These signals travel at considerable speed, as fast as 200 mph, to the brain. We say things happen 'in the blinking of an eye' to measure a short period of time.

Many of the actions of the body are this kind of reflex action, which are usually involuntary, but some can be stopped, or inhibited if we wish to do so. The knee-tapping test used by a doctor prompts a reflex action and from variations in the knee jerk reflex he can tell if there is anything wrong with the central nervous system. The baby coming to grips with his world depends on reflex actions to survive, although he may later learn to control or do without some of them.

The idea of inhibition is essential to many kinds of control. It is often necessary to stop something happening in order to allow something else to happen. In muscular movement contraction of one set of muscles must be accompanied by the relaxing of an opposing set or no movement can take place. So some of the nerve fibres taking messages to the muscles are inhibitors.

The brain is known to have rhythmic cycles of activity, and through these the mass activity of nerve cells in the cortex can be studied, using an electrical recorder called an electroencephalogram, which draws a graph of the brain activity on a pen recorder. The real nature of these activities is unknown as yet. Known as Berger rhythms after their discoverer, the wave patterns are as exclusive to the individual as fingerprints. A received sensation can stimulate the rhythms or inhibit them. In sleep they slow down, but hypnotism has no effect on rhythmic activity.

Annoyance can be shown to stimulate theta rhythms, 4—7 oscillations per second, while the normal alpha rhythm, at 8—13 oscillations, is reduced in amplitude if the individual is concentrating on a problem or paying attention to something. However, we are still a long way from understanding the complex activities of the human brain.

The community of cells we call a body needs other control systems which act in response to messages from the brain, but in a different way to the central nervous system. At every level of existence from protozoon to human body there are feedback mechanisms involving cells, tissues, glands, organs and other living organisms. All living organisms consist of cells, of many specialized types. The health of the organism depends on each cell doing the right job at the right time, a process controlled by the endocrine system. Whereas the nervous system requires a quick response and stops when the stimulus ends, the endocrine system is slow acting and its effects persist for long periods. The two often act together.

The endocrine system sends messages from the glands, using messenger hormones which reach every cell of the body. Each gland controls specific cells so that a hormone is not selective in its delivery. Only those cells which need to respond to a particular message do so. The messages take some time and their effect is long lasting.

The controlling gland is the pituitary which is attached to the brain. The hypothalmus, which is the switchboard of the brain, receives both nerve and chemical messages. It sends out messages

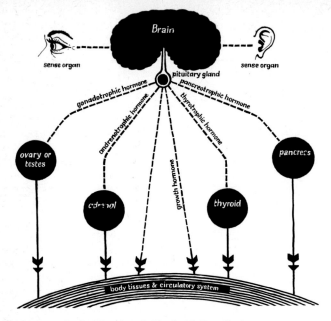

The hormone-gland system controlled by the pituitary gland

in two ways, by impulses through the nerve network and by hormones to the pituitary gland. These hormones travel along the inside of the nerve axons, so that there is a close association between the two systems. When information enters the brain as nerve impulses and the response is hormone secretion the cycle is a neuroendocrine reflex.

All cells are in a constant state of change, either growing or decaying. It is interesting here to consider what we mean by existence, for we generally think of ourselves as separate from our environment and having an independent existence from our surroundings. Yet all living organisms are continuously exchanging material in reaction with their surroundings. We eat, drink and breathe to live. If we eat or drink the wrong things the body becomes disordered and can die; if we fail to get enough of the right chemicals then skin, bone or muscle deteriorate, we suffer from diseases like scurvy and rickets, or starve to death.

So we retain our distinct identity only by taking the atoms and molecules around us and transforming them into the cells which build our living form. This ordering process is called negative entropy, since entropy increases as the system becomes more disorganized and decreases as order is restored. The pages of this book have low entropy as long as they remain in page order. Tear them out and their entropy or disorder increases, but can be lowered. Throw them from the window and their entropy increases to the point where any order or organization ceases. To maintain life, then, the body must remain organized and so maintain a state of low entropy, by interchange with the environment.

Examples are abundant in the natural world, where feedback and control operate in natural and social systems, on a scale of size and time much larger than those of human or machine. The ecology of a natural region, the economic and political structure of a nation can be described in cybernetic terms.

The hunter and the hunted maintain a precarious balance in ecology, and the interdependence of plants, animals and insects is sensitive to changes of climate or the import of external modifiers, like insecticides, weed killer and other human intrusions.

A natural ecological region where climate, plants, insects and animals hold a dynamic balance of related food chains and life cycles. Buffalo in the Kruger National Park

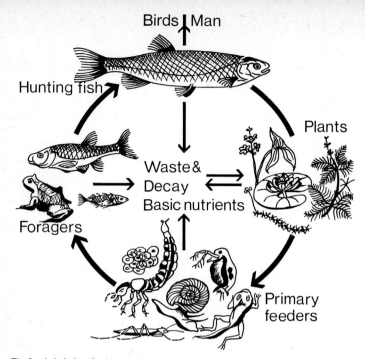

The food chain in a fresh water habitat. There is a large degree of interdependence and competition for food, or avoiding capture, and living space

Left in its natural state a geographic region and the life forms that occupy it will maintain balance or adapt to changing influences, like climate. An increase in one population, the prey, provides more food for the hunter. Its population in turn will increase and feed more heavily on the prey to decrease their number and so reduce the food available. This cycle goes in generations with a time lag that leads to instability if taken in isolation, but there are so many interconnected cycles of growth and diminution that a balance is maintained until some external variable upsets it. The ecology will then establish a new balance which compensates for the intruding factors.

In recent years we have become uncomfortably aware of the effects of man's intrusion into natural processes. Pollution and interference with the ecology have produced radical changes in animal population, plant life and to the climate of whole regions, to the extent that human life itself may be threatened. The presence of detergent, oil and chemical wastes in water can wipe out whole fish populations, with subsequent changes in the rest of the life

Detergent foam on canal water—such human pollution can drastically upset the balance of life cycles and have far-reaching consequences

cycle of which they were a part. Dr Kai Curry-Lindahl, describing the problems of animal conservation in Europe, wrote, 'Today very little remains of the past forest abundance in Europe. The transformation from virgin forest to cultivated woods, vast crop monocultures, industrial areas and big cities is the most radical change of nature that has struck Europe since the last glaciation. Its impact on animal life is obvious.' He then describes the decimation or total extinction of a number of animals—Polar bears, walrus, Harp seal, Monk seal, wild reindeer, Spanish lynx, bison, otter and many others. Having flouted the rules of cybernetics, from ignorance, greed or apparent necessity, we are now having to apply them on an international scale to conserve our own lives.

The interaction between man and machine is the aspect of cybernetics which most directly enters our daily life. Whether driving a car, using a computer, operating a factory or sending a satellite into orbit man assumes the role of ultimate controller in deciding how the machine will operate. We communicate with the machine, and in so doing use it as an amplifier of our own abilities, either by direct operation, as in steering a car, or through automatic systems which we can instruct and from which we receive results in return.

This man/machine interface allows complex control situations which man alone could not handle. Here automatic systems do the 'intellectual' acts of making comparisons, selecting the best solution, allowing for variations in external stimuli and adjusting action in response to them.

We can substitute computer for man as the controller, and use its high speed and large memory where we could not react quickly enough, or continuously, in response to information. The most dramatic illustration of this interaction was the return from space of the crippled space vehicle, Apollo 13, after its own internal systems had been damaged. The complex assessment of new flight paths, precise adjustment by rocket motor burns and many other adaptations to the new conditions could only be accomplished by highly developed control and communication systems.

In the business world this same man/machine interface is affecting the very nature of our society. Industrial products have a life cycle, through research, design, production and use, which is a hierarchy of feedback systems resembling an organism in their complexity.

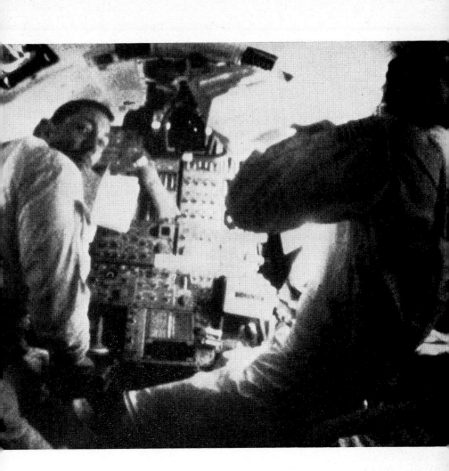

Astronauts Haise and Lovell check equipment on the crippled command module of Apollo 13

The business organization must continually adjust to changing markets, fluctuating supply and financial restraints. Design and production, the long sequence of connected operations from design requirements to packaged product, are becoming automatic. The man/machine control, in which measurement, adjustment and final accuracy were the operator's responsibility, is replaced by control sequences which go through all the processes automatically.

Continuous processes, chemical and petroleum plants, can be simulated on a computer and their processes regulated to precise criteria. In producing discrete components there is a repetitive element which can be programmed. The design process then becomes one of defining requirements and constraints, writing the program, using computer techniques to optimize the design and feed it directly to the production line. Each stage in manufacture can then be centrally controlled. The computer can take account of the external conditions and keep to set standards of accuracy. There is a high degree of flexibility, since one machine can deal with a variety of jobs.

Automation is thus the application of cybernetic processes to production control, in the widest sense. This change in the character of work is having a profound effect on the nature of our society, and our concepts of work and leisure.

The fluid catalytic cracking plant of a refinery producing high octane petrol and by-products. A complex real time process control situation

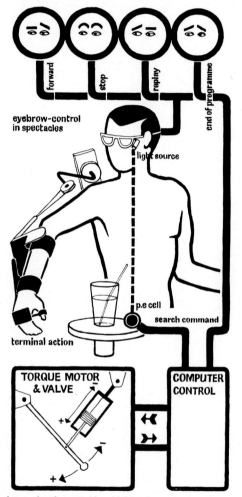

One form of myo-electric control in which eyebrow movements control artificial hand movements

If machines can be built to imitate the activities of man's senses and limbs, could not the methods be used to help man himself? A lost sense or limb is a severe handicap to man. Cybernetic principles can be used to provide substitutes or prostheses, which can be controlled by, and sometimes built into, the human body.

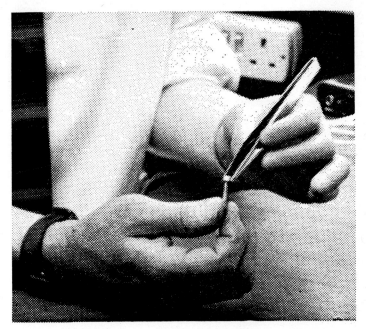

Accurate control of artificial hand to produce precise and delicate movements

Servosystem within the hand to provide muscle action

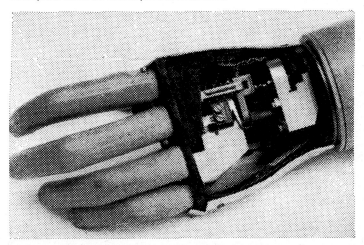

Wiener foresaw the use of cybernetics for prosthesis, and McCulloch in 1947 developed a device for using hearing as a replacement for sight in enabling the blind to read. In 1960 Kobrinsky in Russia demonstrated myo-electric control which uses the electric potentials of muscle contraction to produce the control signal, and today several centres are developing the method. The controlled contraction of any muscle can be used to activate servomechanisms by sensing the electric potentials generated. Since movement is slight the body itself need not move so the principle can be used in restricted conditions or by paralysed patients. An artificial hand using this principle, would sense signals within the stump and so be precisely controlled to perform actions similar to those of the human hand it replaces.

The microminiaturization that we saw in computers is also being found valuable in prosthesis. Implanted sensors, batteries and artificial muscles can be used to assist or replace damaged and failing parts of the human body.

For our external senses too electronics and engineering are providing new kinds of aids, ultra-sonic torches and glasses for the blind are a step towards the direct stimulus of the cortex of the brain which recent experiments suggest may be possible. A group of sensors, scanning a printed page, could relay sufficient information for the message to be 'read'. This is a direct application, unlike previous methods which substitute one sense for another, as Braille uses touch to replace sight.

From imitating limbs and senses it is only a step to make machines which imitate man himself. We have seen the problems in attempting to reproduce the activities of the brain and central nervous system, but machines can be made to perform relatively limited tasks.

So the walking statues of Antium have their utilitarian equals today in machines designed to do the work of men by imitating their actions. Popularly called robots these tools use systems of sensors, processors and actuators to carry out a program of work. Like learning machines, to which they are related, they have only a limited ability to do the work for which they are designed. In

The science fiction robot made reality at Expo 70 in Japan. 'Where amicable robots snap photographs, stamp cards and perpetuate each other with spine-chilling efficiency.'

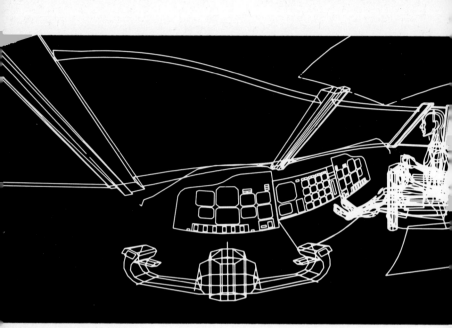

Boeing computer graphics. The animation of the human figure by computer, with film sequences showing movement of various limbs, used in studying cockpit instrument location and ease of control

industry such machines are doing jobs in dangerous and hostile environments that the human being cannot tolerate, and performing repetitive tasks. Just as the computer has extended the mind of man, so these automatons can extend his body, as all his tool-making attempts have done.

In the twenty years since its christening, cybernetics has influenced almost every aspect of our lives. Between men and machine the dialogue is becoming more direct, from simple control

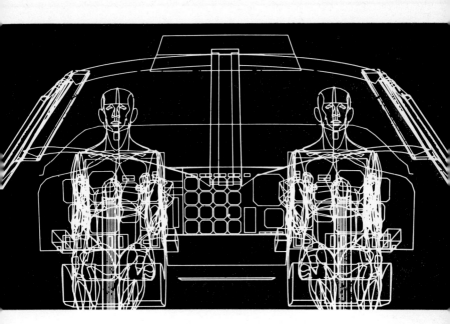

we are now reacting to new knowledge and to a creative use of the facilities we have acquired. Man can visualize his ideas at the moment of creation, and test them without the labour of repeated approximations. He can apply all the information at his disposal and devise from it the specific solution to his problem. He can explore ideas with as much facility as he can make objects or control environments. He can create and control to an extent that was not before possible, in the creative arts no less than in the

The computer as a creative tool is being used increasingly for drawn images, traditional and formal, and in new ways to create motion or control environments. *Verifying Star*, Donald K. Robbins: three-point star used to check plotter functions, superimposed on itself

practical, and it is to be hoped that the knowledge is used with wisdom to improve the human lot.

The evolution of society today depends on the right use of the tools of control and communication it has developed.

Society can only be understood through a study of the messages and communication facilities which belong to it, and in the future development of these, messages between man and machine, machines and man, and between machines, are destined to play an ever increasing part. (Norbert Wiener)

Bibliography

I.Adler *Thinking Machines* London: Dobson 1961; New York: John Day 1961

A.M.Andrew *Brains and Computers* Toronto: Harrap 1963

Stafford Beer *Decision and Control* London: Wiley and Sons 1966

Edmund C.Berkeley *Giant Brains* London: Wiley and Sons 1949

Jeremy Bernstein *The Analytical Engine* New York: Random House 1963; London: Secker and Warburg 1965

Robert Borger and A.E.M.Seaborne *The Psychology of Learning* London: Penguin 1966

V.H.Brix *Cybernetics and Everyday Affairs* London: David Rendel 1968

Emile Caillet *Pascal—The Emergence of Genius* New York: Harper and Row 1961

J.Cohen *Human Robots in Myth and Science* London: Allen and Unwin 1966

R.B.Davison *A Guide to the Computer* London: Longmans 1968

Norman Feather *Mass, Length and Time* London: Penguin 1959

Donald G.Fink *Computers and the Human Mind: An Introduction to Artificial Intelligence* New York: Doubleday 1966; London: Heinemann 1968

Martin Gardner *Logic Machines and Diagrams* New York: McGraw-Hill 1958

S.Handel *The Electronic Revolution* London: Penguin 1967

S.H.Hollingdale and G.C.Toothill *Electronic Computers* London: Penguin 1965

Maboth Mosely *Irascible Genius, A Life of Charles Babbage, Inventor* London: Hutchinson 1964

Robert W.Marks (editor) *Great Ideas in Modern Science* London: Bantam 1968

Jean Mesnard *Pascal—His Life and Work* London: Harvill Press 1952

Philip and Emily Morrison (editors) *Charles Babbage and his Calculating Engines—selected writings* New York: Dover Publications 1961; London: Constable 1961

Brian Murphy (editor) *The Computer in Society* London: Anthony Blond 1966

John von Neumann *Computer and Brain* Yale University Press 1958

J.P.Pfeiffer *The Thinking Machine* Philadelphia: Lippincott 1962

J.Rose *Survey of Cybernetics* London: Iliffe 1969

J.M.Rosenberg *The Computer Prophets* London: Collier-Macmillan 1969

Jagjit Singh *Great Ideas and Theories of Modern Technology* London: Constable 1961

Sara Turing *Alan M.Turing* Cambridge: Heffer and Sons 1959

M.D.Vernon *Psychology of Perception* London: Penguin 1962

A.Vorwald and F.Clark *Computers* London: Lutterworth 1963

Norbert Wiener *Cybernetics* (2nd ed.) London: Wiley and Sons 1961

—— *The Human Use of Human Beings* London: Sphere 1969

John F.Young *Cybernetics* London: Iliffe 1969

Acknowledgements

The Story of Cybernetics is based on the display first produced by IBM for the exhibition 'Cybernetic Serendipity' at the Institute of Contemporary Arts, London. The author would like to acknowledge the invaluable assistance of all those who contributed to the display, as well as the collaboration of his colleagues at IBM and the staff of the Science Museum, London. Particular thanks are due to Mr Dennis Mills for his work on the display and for many of the diagrams used in this book.

The author is also grateful to IBM and the Science Museum for contributing a large number of the photographs. Thanks are also due to the following: for the illustration on page 27 to Mr Enzo Ragazinni; on pages 59 and 73 to the Museum of the History of Science, Oxford; on page 120 to the Tate Gallery; on page 125 to HMSO; on pages 129 and 131 (bottom) to Mr David Ash; on pages 130 and 131 (top) to Mr Joost Hunningher; on page 141 to Mr Dudley Gates; on page 149 to *Design Magazine*; and on page 143 to USIS.